Have you ever fantasized about going to an island and starting a new life? Brenda Paik Sunoo and her husband did just that when they left Southern California for Jeju Island off the tip of South Korea. Real life isn't paradise, though, and the dark history of Jeju mirrors some of Brenda's own losses. This is a lovely book filled with wonderful encounters, moments of self-examination and spirituality, and the amusing—but sometimes frustrating—quirks of rebuilding a traditional stone house. If you loved *A Year in Provence* or the fictional *Stones for Ibarra*, *Stone House on Jeju Island* is a must-read.

— **Lisa See,** *New York Times* bestselling author of *The Tea Girl of Hummingbird Lane, Shanghai Girls,* and *Snow Flower and the Secret Fan.* Her next novel, *The Island of Sea Women,* takes place in Jeju Island.

Every now and then you are blessed to read a book that simultaneously lifts and quiets your soul, that makes you feel that you are a better person for having turned its pages. Brenda Paik Sunoo's latest effort, *Stone House on Jeju Island*, is truly captured in its subtitle, "Improvising Life Under a Healing Moon." Every moment we arrive at in life is the first time we have been in that moment, and every act in our life is in some way an improvisation. This truth is laid out beautifully for the reader in this book that like the copper bell in a Buddhist monastery vibrates long after it has stopped ringing. I will never live in the land of eighty-year-old women who dive to depths I will not know, and I will not in my seventh decade build a windswept home on a volcanic mountain overlooking the sea. But in reading this book I will viscerally know this experience, and I am spirit grateful. Ms. Sunoo's tale is told with great simplicity, honesty, and depth. This is the work of a quiet master. I was touched to read it. I am sure I will not be alone.

— **Noah benShea,** philosopher and international best-selling author of *We are All Jacob's Children* and *Jacob the Baker*

Brenda Paik Sunoo's book *Stone House on Jeju Island* documents her transition to her ancestral homeland. It is poetic, touching, funny, insightful, inspiring, and, thanks to her full-color photographs, beautiful.

She describes building a house in a traditional Korean fishing village ("A memory is embedded in every corner of our house"), learning the language ("the market is an interactive . . . dictionary"), and making new friends (eating with people who also experienced losses, she writes, "We could taste each other's sorrow"). Ultimately, you will celebrate when she and her husband learn to live and "let the wind blow and the land breathe."

— **Paola Gianturco**, author of *Wonder Girls: Changing Our World* and *Grandmother Power—A Global Phenomenon*

A wonderfully charming, insightful, and hopeful book about possibilities. I am not likely to build a traditional stone house in a coastal fishing village near the Yellow Sea, so instead I will follow Brenda Paik Sunoo—a wise and lyrical guide. This is the best of travel books, intimate and compelling, with a dash of adventurous home construction!

— **Sharman Apt Russell**, winner of the John Burroughs Medal, author of the forthcoming *Within Our Grasp: Feeding the World's Children for a Better and Greener Future* (Pantheon Books, 2020)

Sunoo challenges us to reimagine our definition of "home." This smooth and lyrical storytelling of a Korean American's search for her ancestral roots reminds us that home is in our heart and spirit. She is the quintessential example of a transnational human being of the 21st century who knows no boundaries and invites us in for a peek.

— **Kenyon S. Chan**, Chancellor Emeritus of University of Washington, psychologist and former editor of *Rice* Magazine

An extraordinary book, wise and wonderful. Brenda Paik Sunoo uses her gifts as a writer and visual artist to piece together a tapestry showing how to take risks as a senior couple and be fully present in each moment. It is Sunoo's poignant love story about creating a new and healing life in one of Jeju Island's traditional fishing villages. Inspired by the granny free divers, she envisions a journey of aging purposefully while "finding the time to slow down and inhale the luster of another full moon."

— **Judith Van Hoorn**, PhD, former Peace Corps volunteer in Korea, Professor Emerita at the University of the Pacific, past president of the American Psychological Association Division of Peace Psychology

This book intimately weaves together the Korean American author's personal experiences of settling and finding consolation on Jeju Island with sketches of the island's history, culture, and lifestyle. There's a rush of publications on Jeju lately, but only a few fully capture the island's charms from a stranger's perspective. This book is Brenda Paik Sunoo's second book on Jeju to follow *Moon Tides*, and as a Jeju Islander myself, I applaud her affection for the island.

— **Kang Young-pil**, executive vice president of the Korea Foundation

Stone
House
on
Jeju
Island

Stone House on Jeju Island

Published in 2018 by Seoul Selection U.S.A., Inc.
4199 Campus Drive, Suite 550, Irvine, CA 92612

Phone: 949-509-6584 / Seoul office: 82-2-734-9567
Fax: 949-509-6599 / Seoul office: 82-2-734-9562
E-mail: hankinseoul@gmail.com
Website: www.seoulselection.com

ISBN: 978-1-62412-116-6 52600
Library of Congress Control Number: 2018957313

Printed in the Republic of Korea.

Stone House on Jeju Island

Improvising Life Under a Healing Moon

Written and photographed by Brenda Paik Sunoo

Seoul Selection

For Jan,

whose partnership of 50 years plays on

Preface

Facing a howling wind, I squint my eyes. The gravity of my own weight is reassuring as it anchors me along Aewol Village's coastal walk. It's the beginning of autumn and the rough waves are shooting salty droplets toward my ankles. Just minutes away from our stone house, I regularly encounter Jeju Island's wind, volcanic rocks, and women of the sea. During low tide, the local free divers, known as *haenyeo*, search for sea urchin, turban shells, and abalone. Whenever I spot them, I feel optimistic and robust. If they can dive well into their eighties, then I have no excuse to mourn as I enter my seventies. This decade shall be endowed with new beginnings.

My husband and I have been coming to Jeju Island every year since 2011. Our stays began as short visits. Jeju, we rationalized, would be our annual get-away destination from the United States. But each year our visits became longer and our relationships deeper. After surviving the sudden death of our younger teenage son Tommy in 1994, I have since navigated my healing journey not only inwardly, but outwardly toward places that bring us comfort and joy.

Although known for its natural and healing beauty, Jeju Island has also survived its own dark history: Japanese occupation, the Korean War, and the mass murder during the April 3 Uprising and Massacre, known as Sasam (or 4·3). Their vulnerability and *han* (suffering)—far greater than mine—resonates deeply with my own loss. I feel most at home in this compact island because it has suffered and endured. It mirrors my inner landscape.

In 2006, I wrote a memoir about grief and healing entitled *Seaweed and Shamans—Inheriting the Gifts of Grief.* My narrative was reflective, rather than prescriptive, because everyone's healing journey is unique. In my epilogue, I wrote "You may wonder after a decade, are we finally healed? If being healed means living your life more meaningfully, and accepting the bittersweetness of it all, I would say, yes. Laughter and joy did return into our lives." But it was not without private moments of regression and tears.

Fast forward to 2018. I surprise myself when I do the math. Twenty-four years have already passed since Tommy's death. I am saddened that there have been more years without him than with him. Since his absence is present every day, I often imagine him more than remember him, and sometimes I feel guilty for that. Even though I don't feel the same piercing grief as before, I still ache with a yearning and a longing for time we were never granted. Events that will never be shared. A future that will never emerge. I think it is natural and human for me to feel this way. So I remind myself often that "comparison is the thief of joy." What is, is.

If I experience something that triggers a memory or epiphany, I am consoled. In Jeju, when I watch the *haenyeo* harvesting seaweed, I am often reminded of two Mrs. Kims, Korean-American mothers who prepared *miyeokguk* (seaweed soup) after the birth of our first son- and after the death of our second son. Each time I am served a bowl of seaweed soup, I recall their generous overture and compassion. When I spot the shadow of a tree trembling on my wall at bedtime, I remind myself that no matter how shaky the tree may appear, it will still be standing upright the following day. Life resumes. The opacity of one's dreams eventually slides into focus.

In 2015, my husband and I began to search for property that would allow us to build a small, eighty-four-square-meter house—one that would be eco-friendly and in accordance with cultural preservation. We found an abandoned, decrepit stone house in Aewol Village, on the northwest coast of the island. What was projected to be a five-month project ended up taking eighteen. We survived a grueling and steep learning curve, never having built a house before, in a country with only Korean-speaking workers.

Now, having lived in our fishing village for two years, we are certain that our decision to live here was correct. Mother Nature's four seasons teach us that following decay and death, there is always renewal. Likewise, building a house required taking risks and having faith that after demolition, we could begin anew and adjust to the ways of this aging traditional community. Having lived overseas once before, we've learned to remain open-minded in our expectations.

Each day is determined less by appointments, and more by serendipity. When I pass a neighborly granny on the road, she sounds off, "Where are you going?" Or another villager notices my grey hair and seeks reassurance, "*Halmeoni*?" You're a grandmother like me, right? When the postman delivers a package, he announces his presence before stepping inside to plop the box on our living room floor. We smile and thank him, undisturbed by what others may view as intrusive. Village life is all too familiar—curiosity simply overriding privacy. My essays herein hopefully offer a glimpse of what I've learned in the course of engaging the landscape, history, and people around me.

Stone House on Jeju Island is organized into three parts. This is because my relationship to Jeju feels as though I parachuted from the sky first, then landed on earth, and eventually dived into the sea. I've tried to capture this descending trajectory by sharing the background of my introduction to the island in "Part 1: Seduction of Wind, Women, and Stone." Then, the decision to build a house in "Part 2: Construction of the House." And finally, our move to Aewol Village in "Part 3: Village Immersion." Lastly, in my epilogue, I excavate more family history of my grandfather, Rev. Yim Chung-koo, who charted this unexpected course back to Korea before I was even born.

While building our house, one of the construction workers seemed perplexed. "Why are you building a new house in a foreign country at your age?" he asked. Why not? Building a house on Jeju Island is a declaration of optimism and hope, even as we grieve the diminishing years of our mortality. It's returning to the womb—a nourishing space to dwell with contentment.

We broke ground on our property during Chuseok, one of Korea's most important lunar holidays. This is when families near and far visit their hometowns to hold memorial services in honor of their ancestors and to enjoy their time together, feasting after the autumn harvest. Life on Jeju Island is like that. Finding the time to slow down and inhale the luster of another full moon. May these stories of an improvised life engage and heal our mutual *han*.

PART 1

Seduction

of

Wind,

Women,

and

Stone

grew up in southern California where the presence of water was as natural and necessary for one's happiness as sunshine. My birthdate of February 13 gives further credence to Aquarius, the astrological water bearer. If I lived in a land-locked area, I would feel as though I were trapped in an elevator. Walking and swimming are two of my favorite activities. But living on an island is quite different than living on the continental edge, where only one side is exposed to the ocean. Jeju, Korea's largest island off the southwest coast of the peninsula, is floating next to the Pacific Ring of Fire—a major area in the basin of the Pacific Ocean where a large number of catastrophic earthquakes, typhoons, and volcanic eruptions continue to occur. Despite these geographic vulnerabilities, I'm still seduced by this tiny island known for its wind, women, and stone.

Over the course of many visits, I began to experience the pleasures of Jeju's varied landscape—Hallasan Mountain, the smaller volcanic cones, the walking trails known as *Olle*, and the traditional fishing villages and harbors. I could envision living here.

But one of my greatest interests was the aging free divers, known as *haenyeo*.* They are assumed to have been free diving for conch, shellfish, and seaweed since before the fourth century. Today, there are approximately four thousand active divers. Over 98 percent are older than fifty and many dive well into their eighties. Before their families began cultivating cash crops such as tangerines and carrots, the *haenyeo*'s earnings were their main source of income.

In all matters, the *haenyeo* continue to live purposefully until they die. If it weren't for these women and their ability to survive their harsh volcanic environment, I would not have adopted this island as my current home. Jeju Island is about possibilities and living in cadence with the mountains, farmlands, sea, and women divers. Together, they are my fiercely-spirited muse.

---

* After many years of campaigning, Jeju *haenyeo* were officially inscribed onto the list of Intangible Cultural Heritage of Humanity by UNESCO on November 30, 2016. Their recognition was based on their unique free diving techniques, their pre-diving shaman ceremonies for safety, and the folk songs they sang as they rowed out to sea. However, these women divers are not only stewards of the sea. They are also fierce patriots. During the Japanese occupation (1910–1945), *haenyeo* staged the largest women-led anti-colonial demonstration in the nation.

Aewol, Moon by the Water

I pinch myself whenever I look at a map of Jeju Island. The mainland peninsula of Korea—bordered by China to the north-west and Russia to the northeast—appears as a westward-facing tiger. Below it, Jeju Island floats in the Yellow Sea like an Easter egg. By choice, the scope of my life has shrunk from ultra-large to extra-petite when my husband and I bought a dilapidated stone house in Aewol, a traditional fishing port village on the northwest coast of Jeju Island.

We didn't intend to buy land, nor build a house. Our original idea was to search for a large two-bedroom apartment with a sea view. But when our friends—natives of Jeju—viewed our options, they wondered: "Why do you need to move so close to the sea? The sea is all around you. If you live too close, your car

will rust. Your windows will be blasted by strong typhoons, and your bones will ache from constant damp weather. Move inland."

Their well-heeded warnings led us to seriously consider what type of residence would be appropriate. What kind of social and cultural environment did we want to inhabit? We could see construction popping up everywhere: new pensions, apartment buildings, cafés, office structures, restaurants. Foreign investors—given permanent residency incentives— were buying land in the mid-mountain areas, creating new colonies of suburban-style homes. Most building projects were being designed in a Western style, changing the indigenous architectural landscape of Jeju Island. Younger mainlanders seeking a better quality of life for their families were fleeing Seoul and moving into the new high-rise apartments in Seogwipo, on the south side of the island.

We viewed this rapid development with sadness. In reaction to the construction boom occurring everywhere, we decided to search for a "*doljip*" (stone house) in a coastal village. Not one within immediate view of the sea, but one within close walking distance. If we were to invest in property, it would have to be something that supported cultural preservation and allowed us to live in a historically embedded community. Having lived in big cities and California suburbs, we wanted to live more simply and in closer harmony with the natural environment and Jeju locals.

The first time I visited Jeju Island in the 1980s, I was immediately attracted to these iconic *doljip* with green, orange, or blue corrugated roofs—its intersecting seams squeezed together like white cake frosting. From higher ground, the rooftops create a colorful patchwork. These days, the traditional dwellings have become more rare and expensive as mainlanders have purchased and converted them into rental units and cafés. So, I asked my friend Youngsook to scan the newspaper ads. In August 2015, she found one listing located in Aewol.

Although this area today is a tourist magnet, Aewol is

located near significant historical grounds. Our village is not far from where Korean military units built a fortress to resist an invasion from Mongolia in the thirteenth century. I try to imagine that the roads I travel by car were once occupied by the Mongols for one hundred years—led by Genghis Khan's grandson, Yuan Kublai Khan, who brought with him 160 horses by ship.

Within view from our port village is Gonaebong Oreum, one of 368 small parasitic volcanic cones that appear like small mountains throughout the island. Along our coastal walking path, there are ancestral gravesites made obvious by the grassy

mounds located in the middle of farmlands. Most villages include a shaman worship area where prayers are offered for the safety of the women divers and fishermen, and for the protection of the people. History and Mother Nature coexist in every direction.

Aewol, like many coastal villages, was established on the basis of freshwater springs. Over a decade ago, some nine hundred of them existed around the island. Ours is named Hamul. Its waters flow from groundwater at the base of Hallasan Mountain, South Korea's highest mountain and revered mythological source of Jeju Island's creation. These springs infiltrate the earth's surface, becoming part of the area's groundwater. The groundwater then travels through a network of cracks and fissures with openings into villages like Aewol, eventually flowing into the sea. Over the years, the literal meaning of Aewol—"moon near the stream rock"—has even inspired poets from the mainland to extol this village's natural virtues.

Elders in our village like my neighbor Kim Jong-ho have strong memories of the springs. They were the center of community life, he recalled, where women gathered water, washed their laundry, and bathed behind high stone walls so the men could not peek. Fifteen years ago, the spring's entire structure was demolished. However, five years ago, the village leaders approved a new modern stone structure to provide a public place to relax. A sign reminds users: "No bathing and laundry." Mr. Kim misses the original stones. "I don't like the way it looks today," he said. "The walls are lower, and there are no original stones. They used to be very shiny and smooth because the women beat the laundry on the stones with their wooden sticks."

Today, children playfully dip their oblivious toes in the spring water. Had I not spoken to the elders, I wouldn't have appreciated that each ripple echoes the invasion of Kublai Khan some eight centuries ago.

Generosity of the Sea

I spotted a turban shell underwater, wedged between two rocks. Diving closer, I could hear the metal tip of my hand hoe scraping against stone, trying to grab hold. Anchored in place, I pulled myself closer and pried the shell from its sanctuary. After immediately breaking the water's surface, I gasped for air while holding it firmly in my gloved hand. "Where's the bag?" I shouted breathlessly to my friend Kwangsook, who was diving nearby. We deposited the shellfish in her red net bag, which was already occupied by tiny sea snails. I repeated the dives, each turban shell eliciting a greater desire for more. Later, I pondered what Jeju *haenyeo* have learned from those who've tragically drowned: Know when enough is enough.

The difference between gratitude and greed—life and death —can be determined in an instant. As one *haenyeo* described during a TV appearance: "You have no idea how hard it is to come up when you're out of breath. It's as if my bones were crushed and the ground below caved in. I get so dizzy I almost sink. It's like raindrops in my eyes. . . . The dead in the underworld don't breathe. So some say that diving is like carrying the bottom board of your coffin underwater."

I never experienced this type of physical peril. My entry into the world of free diving came later in life. Most *haenyeo* began diving when they were young teens, following their grandmothers and mothers to the sea. Their ease in the ocean is as comfortable as mine in a bathtub. But I changed that history in 2012. It was a year after I wrote my book *Moon Tides—Jeju Island Grannies of the Sea*. This project was inspired by Jeju's aging free divers, known as *haenyeo*. I wanted to document their lives since they are likely the last generation of indigenous sea stewards.

My husband and I enrolled in a five-month program at the local *haenyeo* school. Established by the son of one of the local divers in Gwideok Village, over sixty men and women—three of whom were foreigners—signed up to learn the basics of free diving from actual *haenyeo* instructors. I was one of the oldest, and certainly one of the least competent. I could barely hold my breath for more than thirty seconds at first. That's hardly enough time to even scour the sea floor. By the time I spotted a turban shell, sea snail, or sea urchin, it was time to come

up for air empty-handed. I rejoiced each time my lips broke the surface of the sea. My friend Youngsook, meanwhile, shot back up with three turban shells in each hand. "How do you stay down so long? And where do you find those camouflaged critters?" I wondered. "Between and under the rocks," she answered with the wisdom of experience.

Natives of Jeju like Youngsook grew up by the sea. As a young girl, she and her friends would swim for hours while their mothers earned money diving. At age twelve, without any lessons, she began diving on her own for sea snails and turban shells. After grabbing her first slimy sea cucumber, her prowess became obsessive. "Every night, I kept dreaming that I would catch the biggest abalone ever!"

But no matter how much I tried, I could never come up to the surface with more than one turban shell at a time. After adjusting the number of weights I wore, perfecting the trajectory of my dive, and securing a face mask that would remain water-free, I thought I would achieve better results. But no. I was still afflicted by a fear of air-starvation. As a novice diver, I often still depend on a snorkel as my sluice gate between the depths and the sky. But a free state of mind is more important than one's gear. If I could learn to breathe properly and relax, then I could befriend the sea at greater depths.

My friend Sherrin, an Australian free diver and former English language teacher, instructed me to practice progressive breathing from the stomach to the diaphragm and chest. "Breathe out for twice as long as you breathe in. Three days and you'll be sorted." Other free divers describe their process in stages: the prep, the descent, the hunt, and the ascent. Each stage is accompanied by an affirmation, metaphor, or visualization. One diver described his relationship to the fear of air starvation as knowing that "it's out there in the consciousness. I physically smile at it like an old acquaintance, neither friend nor enemy."

It's taking me a while to feel that the sea is an old acquaintance. We're still flirting and getting to know each other's true nature. But since I am greatly seduced by its underwater beauty and fearful of its wrath, I will continue improving my breathing skills and lung capacity so I can dive for longer periods of time. When I do acquire the level of relaxation and confidence to pluck an abundance of shellfish, may I be as mindful as the wisest *haenyeo*. Prudence must prevail over greed. Otherwise, there will be no safe ascent, no return to life.

Feet to the Ground

Even though my legs are short, I move very quickly. I suppose it's because I always needed to walk faster in order to keep up with my taller friends. It became a habit, a part of my nature that operated in sync with a rapid-fire brain. The thought of slowing down—and all of its layered meanings—occurred only after I passed the age of sixty and now serves as a well-being mantra for my seventies. I was never a jogger. But I love to walk. And since mobility at my age is one of the greatest blessings of all, Jeju Island is my four-season, can-go-anywhere paradise.

In the past, Koreans primarily viewed Jeju Island as a honeymoon destination. These days, it is considered a place of wellness and healing. Younger and older people greatly enjoy its Olle trails. *Olle*, in the Jeju language, refers to the traditional narrow pathways that connect the street to the front gate of a village house. But today's Jeju Olle trails have taken on a broader meaning, referring to the network of twenty-six different routes that lead sojourners along dramatic sea coasts, through farmlands, villages, woodlands, valleys, and forests.

My husband and I have traveled on most of the trails, by car, bike, or on foot. My attitude, until recently, was to be dismissive of these human-delineated trails. "There are walking paths everywhere in Jeju. Why should I walk along a path defined by someone else?" The moment I felt too tired to continue on a path, I wanted to stop and turn around. I scoffed at the saying: "No pain, no gain."

But my friend Youngsook has walked all of the Olle trails. I envied her stamina and began to reconsider the notion of completing a route and pushing beyond one's physical comfort zone. After all, I've hiked four of the arduous trails up Hallasan Mountain. The more I thought about it, the duration of a route didn't have to define the speed or manner in which one reveled in the journey.

In order to celebrate our matching lunar birthdays, my husband Jan and I decided to walk one entire Olle. We chose Olle trail No. 15 because it included the two villages where we have lived on Jeju Island: Gwideok and Aewol. At 9 a.m. we began the sixteen-kilometer route at Hallim Harbor and concluded our walk at Gonae Harbor in five hours, minus the periodic stops to shake out the gravel from our hiking boots and nibble on our snacks. We didn't rush if one of us wanted to stop and take a photo. We didn't even argue once.

Along the way we smelled the salty sea, feasted our eyes on large fields of green and purple cabbage, stopped at a Buddhist temple known for worshipping penile deities, rested our feet in Nabeup Village, and hiked through the upper woodlands before ending the route at Gonae Harbor via Gwa Oreum.

By the end of our walk we were exhausted, but not in a negative way. While resting on a nearby bench, Jan could think of only one thing. "Let's go to a bathhouse." So we called a taxi and rode back to our car, then headed to the nearest public bath, where we soaked our weary bodies and napped on heated stones in the dry sauna.

The next morning, we talked about our Olle walk and concluded that we should never take our mobility for granted. No matter the number of steps one takes, the point is to take them. As my physical condition becomes more limited or if I should become disabled, I vow to keep on moving. It shouldn't matter if I use a cane, crutch, or lean on someone else's arm for assistance. On Jeju Island, I would have no excuse to remain immobile. Hardly a day passes without seeing a ubiquitous granny bent over and shuffling around the village with her lightweight push cart trolley. Her steps are measured with perseverance and pragmatism, transporting not only purse,

seat pillow, and groceries, but the full weight of her cumulative years. Walk, don't run.

Winds of Hallasan Mountain

Jeju natives love their wind-sculpted nettle trees. They have provided shade, spiritual comfort, play and kinship in villages throughout the island. In times of change and uncertainty, the nettle trees have also been considered trusted souls. They listen quietly—without moral judgment—as villagers share their secrets and ask the island gods for advice or forgiveness. Shamans, who serve as the messengers between two worlds, have also performed ceremonies near the trees, drawn by their healing energy.

On a more practical level, Jeju women had once devised an ingenious water filtering system by placing water jars next to the trees. They catch the rain that pours down the trunk of the tree onto a plait of straw that feeds the water into a collection jar. Since the trees were closer to their homes than the sea, this

method was a more convenient way to collect water.

The nettle tree's slanted appearance is unique. It reminds me of one of my yoga poses—the sideward bend. Due to the strong sea wind that blows against the tree, the branches bend in the direction of Hallasan Mountain—Jeju's mythological origin of the founding Tamna Kingdom. This is why it's easy to identify these trees. Most villages have one or more of them situated in accessible locations. Usually, a resting platform has been built around them so the locals can be shaded from the sun while taking a nap or sitting among their friends. Over the years, one can only imagine how many thousands of stories have been exchanged under the cool shade of these trees.

Because of its beauty, the nettle tree continues to draw the

attention of locals and artists. Even poets from the mainland have been inspired to write odes to the beloved village fixture. When my neighbor, Kim Jong-ho, walks along a row of six of them in nearby Gonae Village, he watches the birds fly in and out of the trees. "They fly in between the branches, never touching the leaves. When humans build cities, they destroy the environment. But the birds preserve their city in the sky," he said.

Some nettle trees are hundreds of years old. As such, they are a major part of Jeju's arboreal roots. In the center of our village we have two nettle trees, and another one on the grounds of our local middle school. During the summertime, the leaves create a shady umbrella for the weary. People gather and the tree is abuzz with the voices of humans and birds. During the winter, even though fewer people gather under the bare trees, the absence of leaves accentuates the beauty of their dark wavelike branches. But where have all the stories gone?

As a writer, I am accustomed to seeing my work in print. But the history and stories of many cultures are only passed down orally. If I imagine all the secrets and confessions exchanged under the nettle trees throughout the island in a single year, I wonder: Did the strong winds that bent the branches toward Hallasan Mountain also carry the stories there so the mountain spirits could protect them?

An Affordable Lifestyle

Let's talk about money. My husband and I share many of the same reasons for living on Jeju Island. But when he describes our lifestyle to his friends, he repeatedly tells this one story:

One day, the air conditioner in my car stopped working. So I took it to our local mechanic to fix the problem. He told me that I either had a leak, or I needed a new condenser. I told him to go ahead with the repair and I would return in an hour. After I came back, he told me that the car was fixed. The mechanic had replaced the condenser. He further explained that he installed a re-built unit in order to save me money. He never asked for my permission, but just assumed that because my car was old, I wouldn't want to pay for a new one. So with the re-built one, he charged me one third of the price I would've paid in the United States. I felt like he was looking out for me, instead of hustling and upselling.

When we lived full-time in California, it seemed we were always discussing—or arguing about—our finances. Seniors have to constantly review and negotiate the most affordable way to live. Unbelievably, the average cost of retirement in the United States has risen to $700,000. Of that number, 35 percent goes to health care costs alone. The sad thing is that most American families won't ever come close to reaching the average cost. And health care is still a privilege, rather than a right for most Americans.

In Korea, health care is viewed as a responsibility of the government to its citizens. It is not a for-profit national business. Cost of pharmaceuticals is carefully regulated. On Jeju Island, we pay what amounts to $50 per month for health insurance. Medicine is probably one of the cheapest health-related costs. My husband once required ten days of antibiotics and pain-killers for a tooth abscess. Three different pills were conveniently clustered together and sealed in individual packets for morning, noon, and night. It cost him $5.

Neither of us takes it for granted that we have the means and desire to live in both the US and Korea. As part-time summer residents of California, we are very much aware of the higher costs of living in the States. Property tax for a suburban

house costs nearly $3,000 per year. In Jeju, the property tax for our eighty-four-square-meter house in a fishing village is the equivalent of $50 per year. Because we still have family and friends in California, we haven't taken the more radical step of living in Korea full-time. As Korean Americans, we are still emotionally attached to both countries.

I really miss California's Hass avocados, but that's about it. It seems like the majority of our Jeju friends have gardens or know a local farmer. So whenever anyone comes over to visit, chances are they will gift a bag of tangerines, persimmons, jujubes, spinach or other commonly shared produce.

The way in which Koreans serve their meals always includes rice, soup, meat, and *banchan,* a variety of side dishes that are usually vegetarian. If you make them in larger batches at home, you can eat them repeatedly at each meal and only change the meat to fish or fowl. I've become a Master Chef of leftovers—recycling what I discover in the vegetable bins into these side dishes, or I throw them into a soup, stir-fry, or omelet. When you've watched farmers all over the island harvesting their crops, one internalizes the meaning of "from farm to table." We save money by eating seasonally and organically by growing what we can in our own garden.

When we entertain at home, it seems I end up spending more money on our grocery bill. Since most of our friends are Korean, we like to serve dishes they may not have tried before. I remember the time I wanted to serve gumbo; I had to order the andouille sausage and special seasonings, such as gumbo filé, online. If it wasn't for the resourcefulness of my friend who knows a local Jeju farmer, I wouldn't have been able to include fresh okra in the recipe—thirty minutes before my guests' arrival.

Eating Korean food is cheaper. A lunch set of rice, soup, meat, and six different vegetables costs about $5—and the restaurant is right down the street. If we're running errands downtown, we can take-out a simple hamburger with a pork patty, shredded cabbage, pickles, and mayonnaise for only $1. My husband's favorite go-to fast food is from a local convenience store that sells spam rice balls, wrapped in seaweed. Price: $1. If you're willing to improvise and abandon urban pretensions, Jeju Island is affordable on a fixed income.

Seldom at a loss for recreation and entertainment, we are within walking distance of the sea, mountains, biking paths, trails, and coastal villages. If we want to reach the other side of the island, we often pack our folding bikes into our used Daewoo Rezzo, which we bought for $3,000, and drive down the coast for a picnic and afternoon ride. It doesn't take a lot of money to stay fit—Mother Nature provides our twenty-four hour, no fee gym. We are all equal members.

Even after vacationing somewhere else in the world, we never suffer from post-holiday blues. Returning to Jeju Island is always arriving at a destination.

PART 2

Construction

of

the

House

I lived in only two different houses growing up in Los Angeles, California. By age nineteen, I had traveled by ship on a student program that floated around the world to seventeen ports in four months. By age nineteen, my husband had lived in Germany for one year as a foreign exchange student. By the time we met in 1967, our unexpired passports defined our common ground. We married in 1969 and have traveled to no less than forty-five countries together and separately. We've also lived in five different apartments and six different houses in the US—California and New Jersey—and one overseas country, Vietnam. Although we still fancy ourselves as global nomads, rooted in a restless desire to experience life and culture outside of our comfort zone, we didn't foresee our recent decision to create a new home and community in our ancestral homeland, especially on Jeju Island.

A Canadian psychotherapist and Jungian analyst, Brian Collinson, suggests this notion of home: "Our earliest home is the maternal womb, and all our subsequent physical homes carry its shades and tones. In mythological traditions from all over the world, our first home is a paradise, and we are ever seeking to return to it."

This symbolism may not resonate as true for many. But strangely enough, as we embarked on our homebuilding project, I became subtly aware that many features, such as the ceiling beams, the use of wallpaper, grass, an outdoor clothesline, and a room of one's own were all features reminiscent of the two homes I lived in as a child and teenager in Los Angeles. Living in a village among the elderly also reminded me of growing up with my maternal grandmother. Was I seeking to return—in classic Jungian terms—to my childhood paradise?

Whether or not this is true is only part of the story. Building a house on Jeju Island was primarily a human experiment in building cross-cultural relations between client and contractor, between client and workers, and between us and our new neighbors. Given the breakneck speed of Western-style development occurring all over the island, we also made conscious choices in materials and design that would be more eco-friendly and resonant of Korean cultural traditions: Jeju volcanic stones; the heated Korean floor (*ondol*); cedar wood, camellia oil, mulberry paper, red clay, and traditional clay roof tiles. It took nearly a year and a half to complete our contemporary rustic stone house—longer than what was expected.

But slower is better for us aging nomads. We've nowhere else to go. . . for now.

House Spirits

I traveled from room to room with my iPhone's camera. Before demolishing the majority of the abandoned stone house we purchased, I wanted to document the ruins. The torn wallpaper that was curling after being crisped by heat. The crumpled newspaper ad that was stuffed into the clay walls. The sticky spider webs that attached to our hair as we wandered underneath the low ceilings. Anything that would give me a clue about the previous lives inhabited within this vacant space. Is it no wonder that I enjoy watching *CSI*, the crime scene investigation TV series, while fantasizing that I am a forensic expert?

Stepping into what used to be a bedroom, I spotted an ink brush painting of a monk. There was a poem written in Korean, a red stamp in stylized Chinese characters, and the classic Zen infinity circle. The edges were torn and stained. But most of the thin mulberry paper, *hanji*, was still intact and loosely attached to the wall. I gently removed it for safekeeping until such time I could restore and display it like a time capsule in our new home.

Before I learned anything about the poet, I learned more about the family that lived in this house. It was a family with seven children, one of whom was a Buddhist monk. I suspect it was that particular son who was inspired to paint a monk and include this excerpt from a well-known fourteenth-century poem:

> Mountain tells me to live in quietude.
> Sky tells me to live with innocence.
> Abandon greed and hatred.
> Live like water and the wind
> until you depart.

Nearly a year later, our friend Won Changhee confirmed that the author of the poem was Naong Seonsa (Zen Master Naong), a fourteenth-century monk. Months passed without much thought about the painting. But once we had moved into our house, I immediately retrieved the painting. It was loosely folded and carefully stored in a drawer in the apartment where we initially lived.

I asked my friend Ahn Hyekyoung where I could have the painting made into a Korean scroll. She was among the first people I met when I came to Jeju in 2007 to research the women divers. As owner and curator of Art Space C Gallery, she not only supported *Moon Tides*, but hosted a book party for me when I published my second book *Vietnam Moment*. I knew she could refer me to the most reputable scroll makers in Jeju City. We drove together to her shop of choice. The owner was happy to see her again. "It's been a long time. How's your father?" he asked. Hyekyoung called my attention to one of her father's paintings that was hanging on the store's back wall.

The owner asked me how I would like to exhibit the painting. Because of its simplicity—both visually and text-wise—I chose to have the off-white mulberry paper set against a white background to embody purity. But choosing a color was only the beginning. I then had to choose which subtle design on silk backing would best enhance the painting. Hyekyoung and I picked a very faint floral pattern and chestnut-colored rods to hang and anchor the 41-by-118 centimeter scroll.

Today, the painting hangs on one of our narrow living room walls. It's not the type of art that immediately catches one's eye. It is modest and quiet. But I am pleased when our guests take the time to walk over to it and ponder the poetry of Naong Seonsa. How does one continue to live with innocence, especially at age seventy?

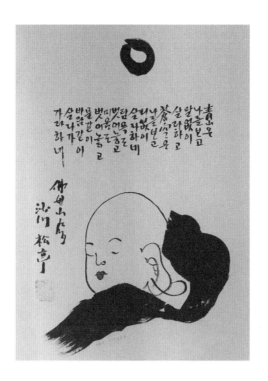

* * *

Before breaking ground, I asked my friend Kang Kyounghee to offer a blessing. I didn't want to upset any spirits that may have been attached to the previous owner. When we first bought our property, it was in complete disarray. I sprayed myself with mosquito repellent each time we had to walk across the yard. I felt itchy just looking at the mess, and yet I fell in love with the ruins and the potential to preserve as much of it as possible. In my mind, the land needed healing and a blessing before summoning the bulldozers.

There were three typical Jeju buildings: the in-law's main house, the married couple's house, and the cow stall. Unlike the main house with stone walls, the smaller unit was not an authentic stone structure, as it was built later with cinder blocks. The size of our property was estimated to be 260 square meters. But the smaller building occupied valuable space that could easily be used as a vegetable and flower garden. Overgrown bamboo leaves lined the stone wall dividing our property from the next door neighbor's house below. What had once been a garden was now a field of weeds and unkempt shrubs.

I asked Kyounghee, who teaches sacred circle dances, to lead a ceremony for us in Aewol. She had spent several years attending international gatherings in Mexico, the US, and Europe. On a few occasions, I participated in such dances at her home in Jeju. The steps are simple enough to learn after a couple of repeated attempts. We always joined hands, sometimes moving forward, backwards, stepping to the left, crossing over our feet, raising our arms in unison. Each dance pattern is paired with a musical track that comes from different parts of the world: the Balkans, the US, Turkey, Hungary, Ecuador, and other places. I requested a song from Hawaii, thinking tropically.

There were only six of us: me, Jan, Kyounghee, Keun (her husband), my friends Soonja (a persimmon dye master), and Youngsoon (the owner of a nearby café). I was asked to include a few significant items that we could place in the center of our circle. I brought a copy of my book *Moon Tides*, a strand of camphor-scented mala beads, and two persimmons. We intended to light a candle, but the late afternoon breeze kept snuffing it out. It was a very quiet and private ceremony befitting our maiden voyage as villagers. Holding hands with our close friends, we moved together in a sacred circle, oblivious to the mosquitos feasting on our blood.

Floor Plan

Most homebuilders hire an architect and a contractor. In our case, we only hired the latter. The house that we bought—and idealistically believed we would renovate—had a living room, two bedrooms, a kitchen, and a hot water boiler room. The bathroom was a country outhouse with a urinal and squat toilet. My husband, Jan, thought it quite charming, in a village kind of way. "We can always use a second bathroom," he initially argued. "Well, don't expect me to run outside and pee during a typhoon," I argued back. After much debate—and lobbying among my friends—he finally conceded to knocking it down.

Our floor plan for the rest of the house seemed simple enough. Re-arrange the two bedrooms and add a modern bathroom with a rainforest shower head and a Korean toilet seat with a push-button bidet. We hadn't even begun to think about the network of cedar beams, walls, and windows. Nor the former cowstall that would eventually become my estrogen cave.

In order to draw up an agreement, our contractor, Mr. Moon, asked to see our design plans. All we had at the time were crude pencil sketches and photos of the existing structure. I liked his decisiveness and his perspective on space. I asked if he was familiar with Korean geomancy, a cultural offshoot of Chinese feng shui. "A little," he acknowledged.

I wanted reassurance that the entrance to the house faced south in order to optimize natural lighting. Koreans believe that everything eventually returns to its natural state. So many features of a house are flexibly designed, such as our mulberry paper sliding doors. If the wood rots, or a child punches a hole through the paper, it can easily be replaced. My calligraphy teacher in the US had also reminded me that whatever I do with our house, keep the design open and furniture low.

Meanwhile, we went home to work on our design plans. The total area of our house would be approximately eighty-four square meters. We agreed not to have any Western-style queen-size beds. There wasn't enough space for that. We would either sleep on the floor, or sleep on our futons. We also agreed that my husband would have an office/music room with the space gained after the smaller building was demolished. With very loose parameters, Jan disappeared into his makeshift workspace in our apartment in Gwideok Village where we

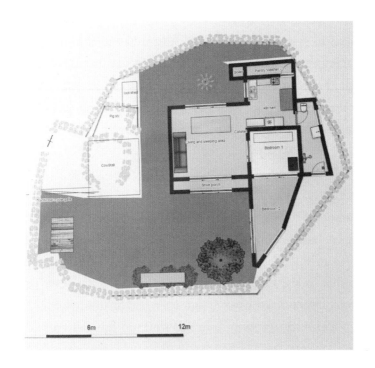

6m   12m

temporarily lived.

A few hours later, he came out to show me a sheet of paper, smugly waving it in his hand.

"Hey, look at this! You won't believe what I just created."

He laid the paper down on the table. "Floorplan.com, baby!" What lay before my eyes was a professional looking floor plan, in color, and replete with exact measurements for the room, windows, and walls. "See here? I was even able to put in those trees, flower beds, and flagstones. Pretty cool, eh?"

"It gets even better! Do you want to view it in two dimensions or three? I can even insert Asian sliding doors."

Truth be told, our contractor was also a very good designer in his own right. Between the two of them, I was confident we could use Jan's floorplan as a baseline to itemize costs and use it as a reference for all further discussions. For the most part, that was the case. But once construction actually began, we relied less on the paper version and our contractor began sketching directly on the cement foundation with a piece of chalk.

We had to make many decisions on the spot. For example, our property line on one side was actually beyond the stone wall that separated our house from the neighbor's. Did we really need to knock down the wall to claim an entitled foot just to grow a few more vegetables? No. The property line on the east side of our land was at an angle. Our bathroom would have to be designed in the shape of a trapezoid. Was that OK? As long as the space widened as one entered the room, we were fine with that asymmetrical feature. Jan's office also wasn't in the shape of a perfect square or rectangle. It would have five walls, including the sliding mulberry papered doors. He would have to get used to placing his desk at a thirty-degree angle from the couch. "As long as I face Hallasan, I'll be happy."

Today, there are so many do-it-yourself apps that give homeowners control over their projects. Jan is still proud that we never paid for a professional architect. That's not to say that he doesn't understand the necessity for them, especially with larger projects. But after spending hours thinking about the size, shape, direction, and purpose of each room, he deserves to boast about his architectural considerations.

When it came to interior design, Jan graciously stepped aside. But our contractor wasn't shy about expressing his own design ideas either. After I chose a glossy tile for the bathroom, he strongly nixed the idea. "It's too seventies," he said.

"Aquamarine is a great color. It reminds me of the Jeju sea," I said.

He listened, then picked up another sample. "Here's a tile, same color, but with more texture."

We agreed on the choice. Now when visitors walk through our house, the bathroom receives the most compliments.

Floorplans are fundamental to space planning. But when it comes to interior decorating, I swear by Let-The-Wife-Decide. com.

Mr. Moon, Our Contractor

When choosing our homebuilding contractor, we were blessed. The first referral never answered the phone. Another was a minister. I definitely knew that I didn't want a minister building our house. If members of his church called upon him to bury the dead or officiate a wedding, it's clear what would be his priority. I preferred someone who wielded a hammer instead of the Bible.

My friend Kyounghee knew we were interested in traditional stone houses. So she asked the owner of a renovated house-turned-café for the name of her contractor. We set up an evening meeting at the café, and that's when we first met Moon Jeong-hwan. I often trust my first impressions. He was prompt and swift in his moves. Agewise, in his late forties. In addition to his expertise in stone houses, I wanted someone whose

aesthetics were rooted in Jeju tradition, but contemporary in execution. I took notice of his premature strands of grey hair, salt-and-pepper mustache and chin whiskers. They indicated a person with confidence and unique style in his appearance. "He's handsome," one of my female friends observed.

When I showed him a photo of the dilapidated two buildings, he immediately said to demolish the smaller cinderblock building. It was not an authentic remnant of Jeju stone houses. I admired his sight-unseen decisiveness to create more space on our property. "Too claustrophobic. Let the wind blow and the land breathe," he said, brushing one arm through the air. Interestingly, the name of his company is Muhan, which means "infinite space."

It took only a couple of more meetings, carefully going over the contract line by line in Korean and English, before we signed the papers and leapt into the unknown. In terms of design, he set our expectations for the collaboration: 70 percent our ideas and 30 percent his ideas. It was reassuring to know that he would respect our ideas, but intervene when we didn't know any better. And there were plenty of those instances. One of his clients said that his prices were fair, and that whatever work he could do himself, he would carry out in order to save costs. In other words, he could roll up his sleeves and do more than carry a clipboard. Jan and I both liked his character—his ability to listen and think before acting. He also expressed a subtle sense of humor. When I asked if we should put a lock on the converted cowstall, he replied: "Well, only if you're going to hide expensive jewelry in there."

Through no fault of his own, what was initially predicted to be a half-year project ended up taking a bit over one year. Competition for workers, unpredictable weather, an unforeseen typhoon, the tangerine harvest season, a dearth of materials, and the Lunar New Year were acceptable—albeit frustrating—reasons for multiple delays. And then there were those that we will never know or understand.

The most unexpected explanation for delays was *singugan*,

a cultural tradition that translates as moving season in Jeju. As a shamanist-based island, locals often defer to the gods when making life choices during important periods. *Singugan* occurs according to the lunar calendar, five days after the coldest day of winter, and three days before the first day of spring. It usually lasts about a week. During this period, the 18,000 goddesses that watch over Jeju return to Heaven to submit their earthly reports to the Great Jade Emperor, who replaces them with a new assembly for the following year. Jeju islanders move at this time so they don't upset the divinities while they are on terra firma. The best analogy is the Western proverb "When the cat is away, the mice will play."

How this cultural tradition impacted our construction project was that workers were too busy elsewhere relocating and settling locals into their new dwellings. What were we? Chopped liver? Without patience, enlightenment, and humor, we wouldn't have finally reached our end goal before the new Lunar New Year in 2017.

As in all matters, the bottom line is communication. If we were building a house in the United States, there would be no language obstacle. In this case, neither of us were fluent in Korean. But I fancied my conversational level as "beginning intermediate." Mr. Moon didn't speak any English so we didn't make a single phone call to each other for the entire year. There was also the cross-cultural dimension—Western-style

communication being direct vs. Asian style being indirect. I would have to find ways to reconcile these differences so we would be on the same page throughout the course of construction. We could not bother, nor depend on, our English-speaking Korean friends every day of the project.

One of the most useful tools was KakaoTalk—Korea's most popular free mobile instant messaging application for smartphones. Mr. Moon and I exchanged IDs so we could use it whenever necessary. It worked well because our messages were written, and I could always use a dictionary. It would satisfy my need to contact him and express all of my obsessive concerns. Since he came from a high-context culture that valued implicit communication, I could easily spare him the frustration of second-guessing us by being as transparent as possible. He would never be clueless. We could also respond at our own comfort and convenience. I often sent him messages in Korean after translating mine from English via another application. "Can we use clay tiles for the roof?" "Construction site empty except for cats (with an added emoticon). Will work continue next week?" "See photos above. What do you think of these bathroom fixtures?" "Skylight installation—when? Rain next week."

Before I sent any messages, I would double-check my Korean translation with Google Translate to save face from any embarrassing remarks. On one occasion, I started my message with an informal "Hi" in Korean. After sending the message, I double-checked with Google that translated my shorthand greeting as "Hey, baby!" Mortified, I checked my Korean-English dictionary again to make sure that Google was wrong, and my Korean was correct. Thankfully, my short-handed greeting was correct.

Most of the time Mr. Moon would write in brief Korean phrases. I appreciated his keeping his messages simple: "Coming in ten minutes. Picking up lumber." "Do you like this door?" "Meeting Saturday." Over the course of one year,

I would acquire a long list of construction vocabulary: installation, roof, foundation, cement, lumber, estimate, main door, etc. I would also learn a few popular Korean phrases, such as "Fighting," which was equivalent to "Go for it" or "Right on!" Who needed to take language classes? I had created my own.

Even the indirect cross-cultural differences came across through KakaoTalk. If I didn't hear back from him right away, I learned to interpret that as "I'm working on it." Or if I asked a yes/no question, no reply meant the obvious. If he said a delivery would occur on Monday, I interpreted that as "Monday is the intention, not a promise." I had already been prepared by others who built houses in Jeju. "Jeju people are independent. They have their own ways of doing things. You will never know all the facts. Be flexible."

Truth be told, I never expected to attribute part of the success of our homebuilding venture to KakaoTalk. Of course, when things got complicated and related to costs, we usually called upon my friend Youngsook to do most of the interpreting. Her position as an instructor at Jeju National University seemed to punch-up our credibility in his eyes. They would communicate comfortably in Korean by phone and KakaoTalk on many occasions. But if it weren't for online translators and my portable Wi-Fi, I can't imagine how we would've communicated beyond drawings and hand signals. Our animated KakaoTalk messages are my cross-cultural diary and glossary of building a stone house collaboratively on Jeju Island. One chat at a time. "Thank you, Mr. Moon. Fighting!"

Volcanic Stones

Nothing defines the island's natural aesthetics more than its black volcanic rocks. First-time visitors to Jeju cannot help but notice them everywhere while touring the island. By the sea, porous basalt rocks of all sizes have been fractured, pounded, shaped, or left as discovered to construct natural spring water barriers, shelters for the women divers, round towers to ward off evil spirits, fortresses, shaman shrines, and lookout towers.

In the city, massive statues depicting Jeju's stone grandfather guardian (*dolhareubang*) are situated at the entrance of many major parks, hotels, and cultural centers. Even the smaller pieces of rock have been shaped into oval pumice stones, a modest souvenir to complement the Korean exfoliating mitt.

There is no absence of attraction to Jeju stones, in whatever form. But I have been particularly drawn to the humble stone structures crisscrossing the ubiquitous farmlands, where the low walls are used to divide property. Depending on the season, the image shifts. During the winter, snow-dusted walls frame an abundant crop of fanlike broccoli leaves. During the springtime, the walls frame vast fields of yellow canola flowers. Year-round, our eyes goggle Mother Nature's quilt-like patchwork. An aerial view could easily mistake Jeju farmland as the Aran Islands in the Republic of Ireland. The stone walls of both undulate through the landscape like rolling waves.

Whether standing on mid-mountain farmlands or hillsides, one inevitably will encounter a family gravesite—grassy dome-shaped mounds well-protected by square stone walls. In the past, such hillside stone walls were built by anonymous local stone masons who carried the heavy rocks on their backs, artfully stacking them up one by one. To this day, many walls are still built without cement, as the spaces between the rocks allow the wind to blow through them, thereby keeping the walls from tumbling down. To construct such walls is both a skill and an art—the roughhewn signature of each stonemason.

Before building our house, I read a book entitled *Listening to Stone* by American stone mason Dan Snow. He wrote: "Stone speaks through the hands when a dry stone construction is created because touch, being the oldest of our senses, is most sensitive to its language. . . . A finished construction is a thought petrified. Within a wall are all the moments that created it. They remain there like hidden messages slipped between the stones as they were placed. The finished wall's character is defined by the spaces between the stones as much as it is by the stones themselves."

The stonemasons that were hired for our house were Jeju-born and in their late sixties and early seventies. They usually arrived on the site at 7:30 a.m. before it got too hot. We enjoyed meeting and talking to them in our survival-level Korean. Mostly, we wanted to watch them in action. During Korea's poorer times, there were few jobs available. So many of today's older workers taught themselves how to cut, shape, and assemble the basalt into beautiful examples of rubble masonry.

Imagine a raw pile of basalt rocks in different sizes, weights, shapes, and textures. With hammer and chisel, they begin piecing the puzzle together, usually starting with larger stones and filling in the empty spaces with smaller rocks. The process is both deliberate and serendipitous. Their judgment is imbued with experience and whimsy. Sometimes it seemed as though they were engaging the stone in secret code. Which one of you should I choose? How much of you should I cut? How will I fit you into this space? While bending their knees, they took deep breaths before lifting the heavier pieces with their gloved hands.

"*Eigoo*," shouted one worker in Korean. "Oh my, this one is

heavy!"

"Doesn't your back hurt?"

"No, I'm used to this," he replied, wiping his brow.

The stone masons were required to build a stone wall around the asymmetrical perimeter of our property and reinforce the existing stone walls of a former cow stall, which I converted into a clay-walled room. At one point, three of the stone masons were working simultaneously on separate walls that were to be embellished with stone. Each wall resulted in its own unique mosaic. But together, their cohesion was questionable.

The next day, we returned to the site only to discover that a portion of the walls had been removed. Our contractor sent me a message: "I did it." Apparently, he was not pleased with the initial results. Mr. Moon had a higher aesthetic benchmark and instructed the stone masons to re-do part of the facade. Afterwards, we could see the improvement.

Once the walls were completed, the smaller stones were left strewn in the field. We were able to salvage those we could easily lift and arrange them as borders for our vegetable garden and flower beds. The stone walls of our house and those that define our property are constant reminders that they are part of Hallasan Mountain's mythology and geological DNA. Each rock spans the memory of the volcano's last eruption five thousand years ago and the signatures of Jeju's elderly stone masons, past and present.

By comparison to these stones, I am a young seventy-year-old chipped grain of sand.

Beautiful Wooden Beams

In the United States, I grew up in a home with exposed wood beams. Gazing upwards, my eyes often fixed on the elongated beauty of ceiling joists and rafters. Their natural appearance and craftsmanship were so prominent that it left a lasting impression as a pleasing architectural feature. So when I arrived in Jeju and began taking notice of the traditional stone houses, I was quickly drawn to the renovated cafés and pensions that retained the interlocking web of beams—some of which were over one hundred years old.

In the past, wealthy owners of a Jeju stone house could afford to use expensive wood. Less wealthy owners had to use whatever wood was available and affordable. In our case, we didn't have a choice. We were unable to save any of the wood beams that were part of the property we purchased. They were made with cheaper wood that had already rotted or been ravaged by termites. We could only save the smaller beams of the former cow stall.

Our contractor, Mr. Moon, told us that our beams would be made with Japanese cedar and stained with camellia oil. One of the most prominent species on Jeju Island, cedar trees were used widely to provide a windbreak for the tangerine orchard industry. He assured us that there would be no problem obtaining the materials locally. The challenge would be to find skilled workers.

Construction began on Christmas Day. Santa Claus and his four elves arrived early in the morning. All were well-insulated in their down jackets and knitted skullcaps. As they sat on their haunches Korean style, Mr. Moon sketched the design of the beams with a red pencil on the cement foundation. Because our beams would be heavier and larger than a traditional stone house, he and the team supervisor discussed the required configuration and steps to follow. Given the design of our house, they would have to build different sets of beams to accommodate a roof with multiple pitches.

We watched in awe as they began piecing together the parts. After constructing one set on the ground and then lifting it on top of the house, they decided to abandon such a heavy procedure. Instead, two workers remained on the roof, while the others cut and passed the measured pieces to them by hand. They were young and steady enough to step around the rooftop without falling or being swept off-balance by the wind. Their aerial moves were acrobatic.

As each truss was completed and raised into position, we could see patches of blue sky framed by the angled rafters. Depending on the light, shadows of the beams were cast against the cement walls. They reminded me of the bold strokes of abstract expressionist Franz Kline. It was instant, temporary art. Up to this point of construction, nothing had excited me as much as watching how the beams were constructed. There was beauty in its incompletion and exposure to the heavens.

Considering the precision and deliberation that was requir-ed, the organic nature of the process was a bit unsettling. At one point, construction came to a temporary halt due to weather conditions and other factors. On several occasions, Mr. Moon would shake his head to underscore the complexity of this endeavor. And yet when it was completed, he was the proudest of all. "It's extraordinary. But I don't think I will ever do anything like this again," he said, shaking his head.

Every morning when I wake up, the first thing I see are the exposed beams. Thankfully, we made the right decision not to cover the rafters with a conventional flat ceiling. We weren't worried that given our Korean-style heated floor system, a higher roof might keep the house colder in winter. We wanted to retain as many architectural elements of the traditional

stone houses as possible. As I marvel at each beam, I can still recall the wind-chafed faces of the young workers and the sound of the buzzing saw. I see Mr. Moon and the team of workers lifting the heavy lumber and discussing measurements, and which way to make them all fit together. In fact, a memory is embedded in every corner of our house, as vividly as I can remember the details of my two pregnancies and natural deliveries.

A funny encounter occurred after the beams were completed. An older worker arrived at the house one day to stain the wood with camellia oil. He told me that the oil was so good that people even ate it or used it to beautify their skin. After telling him that I liked the stained effect, he shared his opinion. "If you left it unstained, it would cure nicely on its own and be beautiful for your grandchildren and great-grandchildren." I laughed and responded, "Uncle, look at me. I have grey hair. Does it look like I have that much time to wait? I want the beams to look beautiful now."

Virginia Woolf—A Room of One's Own

I revel in silence. As a writer, I also need to shield myself from distractions. Otherwise, my brain spins like a rainbow-striped whirly top. Space and quietude are precious commodities. In her essay "A Room of One's Own," author and feminist Virginia Woolf wrote: "A woman must have money and a room of her own if she is to write fiction." I don't write fiction, but I'm certain that Woolf would agree that her advice is applicable to writers of other genres, or women in general. As sublime as being a couple can be, individuals still require solitude in order to engage their muse.

Financially, my husband and I have always survived as a two-income family. We both enjoyed and encouraged each other's professional careers. Because I have worked since the age of sixteen and have passed the age of sixty, I've earned a Social Security check as evidence of my longevity in the American workforce. I eagerly anticipate the third Wednesday of every month to re-fill my paltry coffee can. Money of one's own? Check.

After reading Woolf's essay more than twenty years ago, I never looked back. Wherever we moved, I claimed either a room or a portion of the garage as my personal space. But the idea of having a private domain actually originated before I discovered Woolf's essay. While growing up in Los Angeles in a modest two-bedroom house, my father designated a tiny room next to the dining room as his two daughters' "toy room." It was there that we could play with our paper dolls, board games, and stuffed animals. When the room got messy we were expected to tidy it up, organizing our toys on the shelves that he built. I am quite certain that this is how I first learned to de-clutter and classify. The toy room became our private play space. No adults allowed.

When we stumbled upon the dilapidated stone house in Aewol, I was immediately attracted to the cow stall: its web of low wood beams, the two troughs, five stone walls. . . even the steel ring that was set in concrete to tie the remaining grass-twisted rope formerly attached to the cow. I thought about my father, a man who had never read Virginia Woolf. Yet he instinctively knew that his daughters deserved their own space as much as he did. Dad would approve. "This will become my toy room," I declared.

Unfortunately, due to deterioration, the two other main buildings required demolition. In the past, Jeju families built two units on the same property: a main indoor house and a smaller companion house for the younger married couple. The parents usually occupied the former unit until the eldest son married. Then, the newlyweds would switch dwellings with the parents.

Unlike Korean parents from the mainland, Jeju in-laws were more independent and practical. They lived on the same property as their eldest child's family, but separately. Although we demolished the two existing units, we designed our house in an L-shape to include a room as Jan's office.

But if there was any part of our new property that could be preserved and converted into a healing space, it was the three-meter by three-meter livestock shelter. My friend Soonja suggested that I turn it into a red clay room for relaxation and detoxification. As a mineral, red clay produces negative ions through the earth's inherent radiation. Normally, these negative ions are created in nature—mountains, forests, beaches, and near waterfalls. It's no wonder that we feel refreshed whenever we are close to Mother Nature. Now I could also reap the benefits of these oxygen atoms and boost my immune system there. Our friends loved the idea of being able to stop by for a revitalizing interlude.

I also wanted a Korean floor heating system in order to make it a homestyle heated room or dry spa. Other friends suggested using the space as an art studio or gallery. I saw potential in all of the above and more: a room for detoxification, meditation, sipping tea, writing, and storytelling.

As it turned out, my converted cow stall was one of the final portions to be completed. The main house was the priority, of course. Jan was pleased with his large office and window that faced Hallasan Mountain. If he swiveled in his chair, he could view the plum blossom, quince, maple, and red holly trees in the garden that our friends recommended. We selected one for each season. Meanwhile, I created my temporary office in the kitchen and did most of my writing there until the cow stall was completely converted.

To appease my impatience during the year, I watched many YouTube videos extolling the virtues of the tiny house movement. My friends also suggested books I could read about other homebuilders' experiences. I began visualizing how I would furnish the interior with dimmed lighting, sitting pillows, a bamboo mat, textiles, and porcelain teacups. I documented each step of the conversion process: the raising of the beams, the insulation of the walls, the placement of the skylight, the application of the red clay, the heated stone floor, the staining of the wooden door, and the installation of the clay tile roof. Mr. Moon knew how much the cowstall conversion meant

to me. He offered decorative and practical options: "Would you like the clay walls to be smooth or textured? Shall we add plumbing so you can have a little sink?"

By the new year, I was finally able to heat up the floor and initiate the room with my friends. We huddled together as the sun set, sipping mulberry leaf tea and eating sticky rice cakes. The former cowstall—once wafting pungent manure—had emerged newly fragrant with burnt sage and Jeju citrus. Now when I lie on the heated floor in winter and view the clouds through the skylight, I invoke the spirits of my father, Virginia Woolf, and Aristotle who wrote: "Patience is bitter. But its fruit is sweet."

Our Clay Tile Roof

Nothing wreaked more havoc on my mental state—or our contractor's—as the roof's Korean clay tiles, which are called *giwa*. Known for their interlocking beauty and overhanging eaves, this traditional architectural element dates back to circa 1st century B.C. I agreed with my friend Soonja that this feature would be the most eye-catching crown for our contemporary rustic stone house. Elsewhere on the island, homebuilders were using Mediterranean-style tiles, asphalt, ceramic, wood, and metal. Attractive as they might be, we wanted our roof to echo the cultural past.

There were practical benefits as well. Interlocking tiles prevent cold air, wind, and rain from entering a house. The eaves extend outward and curve slightly upwards in order to allow the sun to enter during the winter, and keep the house shaded like a slanted filter during the summer. Korean clay tiles appealed to us not only because of their organic and practical benefits, but their intricacy and design. The circular end tiles, for example, often include an image of a lotus blossom or the rose of Sharon, Korea's national flower. The long, curved tiles often contain the image of two mythical phoenixes flying toward each other with a flower in between. On our tiles, two phoenixes look like they are kissing.

For the most part, we accepted most delays. However, once the plywood boards and insulation were laid to protect the exterior of our ceiling beams, we had to endure six months of unexpected tile delays before all the resources aligned in the universe. At times, it seemed as though a cosmic force was hell-bent on testing our patience. Were Jeju's goddesses sending us a message that we were too stubborn to hear? Jan kept worrying. "What if rain and snow deteriorate the insulation?" I didn't know how to reply when neighbors and friends kept asking, "Still no roof?"

At one point, I nearly gave up. The weather was turning cold. There would certainly be more days of rain and snow as winter approached. Desperate, I sent a text message to Mr. Moon: "If not possible to ship clay tiles from the mainland or get any skilled roofers, I'm open to considering zinc tiles. Time is running out. What do you think?" I didn't really mean it. But in that moment of homebuilder's angst, I figured I shouldn't be too attached to specific outcomes.

Jan kept reminding me, "Don't be rigid. There are alternatives we should consider." Perhaps, if I let go of my obsession for the traditional clay tiles, I would be freed from my agony.

Mr. Moon responded, "I'll think about it." Fortunately, he never gave up on our original idea nor agreed to an alternative.

A month after Typhoon Chaba hit in October 2016—the last explanation given for the delays—all shipments between the mainland and Jeju Island were understandably halted. Obtaining the materials was only part of the equation. There were no available or experienced clay tile roofers to do the job. If there were such roofers on Jeju Island, our small house certainly ranked as their least important project. We were thus required to recruit and fly in three skilled roofers from the mainland to do the installation. Even with materials and human resources in place, it would take four consecutive days of clear weather to complete the work. That's nothing short of a miracle. It felt like we were waiting for the opposite of the Perfect Storm.

I still remember the day that the three workers arrived on the island. Mr. Moon messaged me that they had landed. Out of curiosity, they stopped by the construction site to see the job they were about to undertake the following day. They huddled and shook their heads. One of them told us that if it weren't for the fact that they had flown in from Seoul, they might

reconsider taking the job. Apparently, the unique configuration of our roof and main entrance made the work more laborious than expected.

Things moved very quickly the next morning. The huge truck that was filled with an unbelievably massive load of tiles could not be driven up the narrow alleyways leading to our house. It had to be parked on the main street downtown. Smaller trucks then had to be rented in order to bring the tiles to the yard's front gate. From there, a team of workers proceeded to unload and place the tiles on the field by hand. Once neatly arranged on the field, the workers began the sequence of alternating rows of convex and concave tiles on the roof.

We watched and filmed the long-awaited process, which included securing the ridges with a mixture of mud and cement. While one man stood on the roof, two men stood below. One formed the mud into the size and shape of a bocce ball. He passed it to the second helper who then tossed it up to the co-worker on the roof—their rhythm impeccably executed. When the workers took a break, we provided enough hot coffee and sweets to keep them warm and fortified. "Thank you, thank you," we kept repeating.

The final results were so transformative that I could barely remember what it looked like before. It was still a modest-sized stone house. But with the new tiles, our house suddenly had acquired a more stately presence. Initially I felt self-conscious and didn't know what our neighbors would think. But one by one they stopped by and expressed their approval and admiration. Several months later, we noticed that four other neighbors in our village simultaneously began building or renovating their homes as well. The owner behind us cleaned and painted his concrete tile roof to match our charcoal-colored tiles. "Look, our roofs look the same," he said. "Yes, it looks great!"

Every day I raise my eyes upwards to view the decorative end tiles that line the border of our roof. Each one is embossed with the rose of Sharon, a beloved symbol of perseverance and loyalty. When the flower withers, all five petals fall away at the same time. I wonder if the camaraderie of our village will decay together in the same way? Or will the interlocking clay tiles shatter into pieces and be hauled away as insignificant debris?

PART 3

Village

Immersion

Living in an American suburb versus living in a fishing village are two vastly different lifestyles. Even with our reservations, we yearned to experience the latter. As foreigners, could we build friendly relationships with our new neighbors?

Moving Day in Aewol occurred on June 25, 2016, about nine months after groundbreaking. I was giddy with anticipation. Although the newly-constructed house still needed permanent clay tiles laid on the insulated roof, an entry gate, a coat of paint, and landscaping, Mr. Moon delivered on schedule. It was habitable: We had electricity, water, a functioning kitchen, a bathroom, and access to the Internet.

Since we were only bringing a minimal number of belongings from our small apartment, we didn't hire any movers. It took no more than four trips back and forth in our compact Daewoo Rezzo to haul the basics like pots and pans, condiments, sheets, clothing, towels, and toiletries. In terms of furniture, I had arranged for the deliveries to take place one day before we moved in. Our granddaughter, Jolena, assisted in setting up our household. She excels in her organizational and interior decorating skills. "Grandma, let's hang the painting there," she suggested. "Put the dishes here."

The logistics of moving was nothing new to us. Over the course of our marriage, we had lived in many places, But this move was like no other. We were now residents of a small traditional fishing village, where no one else spoke English and the average age was sixty. After much doubt about our investment, our neighbors were finally happy to witness this once abandoned house—amid a field of rubble and detritus—demolished and resurrected into a contemporary version of Jeju's traditional stone houses. Thumbs up, signaled one neighbor.

Once moved in, we wasted no time in engaging our neighbors—nor they with us. In fact, after our house was built, four of our neighbors began renovating their own neglected homes. We cheered each other on with collective village pride. Regardless of our limited Korean proficiency, they have been eager cultural advisers, storytellers, historians, and gift-bearers.

In our village, a web of small alleys allows locals to meander along more than one path. Houses are clustered, not lined up in a row. Inevitably, someone will pass by the house. One of my friends warned me that in Jeju villages a stranger may come by unannounced. "Can I see your house?" is a common refrain.

In these villages, locals often leave their front doors unlocked when they go out. If a delivery man arrives with a package, he may place the package inside the house. Bolder visitors may tap on your window before shouting, "Anyone home?"

We lock our doors at night, but feel safer here than in the US because guns are illegal. In the past, Jeju was known for this saying: "No beggars. No thieves. No gates."

Although we have a wooden door that encloses our yard, we always keep it open during the day. If we had kept it closed on New Year's Day, our elderly neighbor wouldn't have entered our property and offered the outdoor wooden platform bed that she no longer needed. "Please take this rest platform. I have no room for it. It will be perfect in your yard."

Our nearby surroundings offer a variety of choices for daily exercise. We are footsteps away from strolling by the sea or climbing nearby smaller volcanic cones, or sitting quietly at a nearby temple. On certain calendar days, we often drive to Jeju City or the town of Hallim to shop at the traditional five-day markets. Every week I meet with two friends to share a meal together, do arts and crafts activities, and exchange language lessons in English and Korean.

Immersing myself in the community has given me a sense of belonging. But social inclusion has also given me the opportunity to learn more about the shadows of sorrow that preceded our arrival. One of my neighbors, Kim Jong-ho, has spent most of his life in Aewol Village. He shared his family's experience during Jeju's April 3 Uprising and Massacre (1947–1954). Mr. Kim also told me that the massive stone walls behind our house were once part of a fortress to repel foreign invaders.

On the other hand, I have also learned more positive examples of local history, such as the contributions of Irish missionaries. A revered priest named Father Patrick McGlinchey and Columban Sister Rosarii McTigue established a Catholic church and textile co-op after the Korean War in the nearby town of Hallim. I was fortunate to meet both of them—the former in Jeju and the latter in Ireland before she passed away in 2015.

Living on Jeju Island, one is always prepared for cyclones, such as Typhoon Chaba. Our house is stockpiled with bottled water, candles, ramen, and canned tuna. We've survived a tsunami in Thailand and urban riots and earthquakes in the United States. But never have we woken up to fallen pine trees, broken steel gates, and collapsed stone walls due to the wrath of the wind and rain. In the aftermath of the storm, we took a walk to assess the damage in our village, our mouths agape. The locals were sweeping up the debris, rehanging their steel doors, and exchanging tales, unfazed. They were already accustomed to the normalcy of semi-tropical village life. Whereas we, their new foreign neighbors, walked around taking it all in so as to further belong.

Neighbors Bearing Gifts

Most of the time I've given flowers, wine, linen, or candles as a housewarming gift. In Jeju, one can skip the frills. When visiting a new home for the first time, Koreans are much more practical. Several years ago, I was invited to a friend's new home in Gimnyeong Village. My taxi driver suggested we stop by the local market. I gave him money and entrusted him to pick out something appropriate, like a box of crisp Asian pears, plum wine, or canola flower honey. But no. He returned to the car with a super-sized package of thirty rolls of white toilet paper and a box of powdered detergent.

"What's that for?"

"It's the gift!"

"Really? Toilet paper?"

He explained that when a Korean family moves into a new

house, the guests should express their wish for fine health, luck, and prosperity. The toilet paper, he said, represents the long life and good health. And if lucky and prosperous in the bathroom, the more toilet paper the better! Detergent, on the other hand, represents cleanliness and a fresh start.

So even before we broke ground, I was anxious to know my neighbors. I had heard stories that when one lives in a village, nothing goes undetected. If one starts out on the wrong foot, you risk alienating those who would otherwise watch your back. My friend Soonja—a native of Jeju—took us around to introduce ourselves to the neighbors. She assured them that we were a worthy couple: third-generation Korean Americans whose grandparents supported the nation's independence movement from overseas. My husband had worked for the United Nations. I authored a book about the *haenyeo* and planned to volunteer at the local middle school. We were not squatters, thieves, or rowdy party animals. Our grey hair accentuated her pitch.

It was easy to get to know our neighbors because there are less than a dozen stone houses in our section of the village. Given the intimacy of our social environment, others were able to witness every stage of our year-long construction— from the initial demolition of one cinderblock structure to the conversion of a cow stall into a writer's cottage.

Once we moved into our house, the neighbors began their

parade across the open dirt field. We did receive the classic packages of toilet paper. One package had muffins and bread. Another neighbor brought over a plate of three boiled potatoes on a chipped porcelain plate. It was early in the morning and a perfect addition to our dish of eggs and sausage. The woman across the road arrived at my doorstep, shouting, "Here, here. Anyone home?" I greeted her with a smile, and she handed me a recycled cotton towel—a remnant that I could use to clean my kitchen counter. It reminded me exactly of the type of kitchen rag my grandmother recycled from rice bags when I was a child in Los Angeles, California. One older man walked over on several occasions and handed me plastic bags containing either seaweed, leafy turnips, or corn. He had harvested the corn in his yard, and the seaweed had been gathered during one of his short bike rides to the sea.

In neighborly fashion, we gave them layers of lettuce leaves that we harvested during the final days of summer. One of the grannies wasn't home, so I left the bag with her son. A couple of days later, she appeared at my doorstep. I could tell she was sweating from the heat. She readily accepted my invitation to come inside. "Aaah, it's so nice and cool," referring to the large floor air-conditioner that was set at a very low temperature. "I came here a couple of times already," she said in Korean. "You weren't here, and I wasn't home when you brought the lettuce. Here, this is for you."

After taking a seat in my kitchen, she handed me a plastic container of cabbage kimchi, two plastic bags of frozen seaweed, and two plastic bags of frozen greens. In the tone of a mother, she instructed me to immediately put one bag of the seaweed and one bag of the greens in the freezer, and eat the others right away. "Put the greens in a pan with oil and stir fry it. Add sesame oil and eat it as a side dish. Or just pick on it like this. . . as a snack when you're not very hungry." She went on to tell me that the seaweed was harvested nearby. "It's very good." I could tell it was fresh by the lingering smell of the sea.

"Thank you. My husband and I will enjoy it all."

"Hurry up, put that in the freezer right now," she instructed again, pointing to the greens and seaweed.

This same grandmother came back another day, even more animated than before. She told me that her children were going to demolish her current house and build a two-story structure over the next five months. "I want to give you some of my grass before the field is cleared for construction. You need grass. All you have right now is dirt. Please, take some."

I thanked her for her generosity, but explained that I would have to confer with my contractor. We might have to keep the field clear for further construction, and I didn't want to waste her grass. Later that evening, Jan and I talked about the kindness of our neighbors. Gift-giving—as we often practice it in the US—tends to be a ritual of signing into registries, last minute shopping, credit card purchases, and occasional extravagances. The gifts we had received from our village neighbors were none of that. Each item—the potatoes, seaweed, greens, and grass— all came directly from our nearby land or sea. Their gifts didn't come wrapped in a box, secured with a bow. They were simply carried in the farmers' own wind-weathered hands.

Next Door Neighbor

When we first encountered our property, we were charmed by the notion of living in a traditional fishing village. It was located fewer than one hundred steps from a small port that feeds into a larger harbor with old wooden boats. In the short period that one has to decide whether or not to buy a property, the background of your neighbor is not part of real estate disclosure. You can choose a house. But you can't choose your neighbor.

In the United States, it's possible to live in a neighborhood and not know—or care—who is living next door. But when you live in a traditional Jeju village, it matters. Neighbors can easily view or engage each other because the yards are exposed and separated only by a low stone wall. One morning as I was hanging my laundry out to dry, my neighbor—an older man—startled me. We were standing there face to face, and neither of us knew what to say.

According to neighborhood gossip, the old man next door didn't own the house. He was given permission to live there rent free, and to keep it occupied for security reasons. There is no electricity, only an outdoor spigot. There was a period of time known as the Vacant House Movement, whereby people were allowed to live in vacant houses for five years, provided it was improved through renovations. It's unclear if that was the circumstance of his occupancy. Or if a relative who owned the land gave him permission to stay. In any case, he was poor and lived alone.

On hot and humid days, he seldom closed his front door. Passersby could view him napping, curled up like a child on a straw mat beaten by the day's hard sun. If he happened to hang his laundry or water his garden vegetables whenever we passed by, he bowed politely and greeted us respectfully. We return the greeting. He was always respectful. When his son and daughter-in-law once visited him, he told them to greet us. "Say hello to my neighbors," he insisted.

Whenever I looked out of my kitchen window, I tried to observe his daily patterns. He rode a bike every day to get around. I've seen him by the sea gathering seaweed on a few occasions. His cotton pajamas, socks, and underwear hung on a clothesline strung between his corrugated roof and the telephone pole outside his house. When he shopped, he seemed to buy only what he needed for the day, such as a tiny bag of pork belly slices for one meal.

Sometimes he walked over to our yard with a generous bag of pumpkin leaves, seaweed, corn, or radishes. "Since we are neighbors, we have to be friendly and share," he said. Sharing is a common virtue among Jeju natives. One day during construction, I put out coffee and pastries for our team of bricklayers. The old man walked over uninvited and helped himself to the tray of snacks. The workers didn't say anything. They offered him one of their cups of coffee. I was perturbed.

Unlike my relationship to the women of my neighborhood, he and I seldom talked to each other. He was also shy. One friend advised us to be friendly, but not to encourage his dependency. Other neighbors tended to ignore him. But one day he caught the attention of the entire village. A young elementary school boy was missing and later discovered sitting quietly in his house. He appeared to be unharmed. Hours after locating the student, a group of parents and teachers came by the house to take pictures to warn the other children about the incident. The local police took him away, and we haven't seen him since.

We don't know if or when he will return. For now, his house is vacant. His herb garden no longer provides lettuce or onions. A neighbor who used to know the previous owner once came by and cut down some of the bushes, but left the debris behind.

I called the local administrative office to request removing the trash, but I was warned not to touch anything on the property. "But isn't it a fire hazard," I asked. It didn't matter. No trespassing. So I've had to face this abandoned eyesore for months on end.

If the old man does return, I will consider justice served without further judgment. Across the stone walls, I envision a relationship that will remain cordial but keenly observant.

Mother Nature's Critters

My granddaughter, Jolena, and I had just returned home after a day of sightseeing. We had moved into our newly built house only a week earlier. Upon entering her temporary bedroom, she calmly called out to me. "Grandma, don't freak out, but there's a giant spider on the wall." The expression on her face was serious. Sitting cross-legged on the sofa, her body was stiff. Normally, I am not one to be afraid of spiders. But when she said "giant," I had no idea what size she was really talking about.

"Where exactly is it?" I asked.

"I'm facing it on the wall beside the door."

"How big is it?"

"REALLY big!"

"OK, let me see."

I slowly mustered my courage to walk into her room. The last time I had seen what I considered a giant spider was when my husband and I lived in Hanoi, Vietnam. Above the entrance to our front door—on the inside—I spotted a spider that was six inches in diameter, including the body and eight hairy legs. I was home alone and had no idea if this air-breathing arthropod was the type that injects venom into its victim. Would it dive onto my head while I ran out the door beneath it? Obviously, I survived that encounter when a neighbor I had summoned in a panic came to my aid with a broom and swept it away into the street.

In this case, I wasn't alone. It was just me and my grand-daughter. Jolena was clearly stunned and frightened. Without much hesitation, she gathered her belongings and fled the room. I could tell that between the two of us, I would be the designated—but reluctant—assassin. Or, at the very least, I had to be the one who remained calm, contrary to what I would normally do if my husband was home. My first reaction would be to scream hysterically and flee the house with my cell phone to call him later when the coast was clear.

"We need to think strategically. We can't squash it on the wall. It will leave a gooey mess on the new wallpaper," I said, adding, "It's mulberry paper."

After a brief discussion—outside the room—we decided that I would brush it off the wall with the broom; Jolena would then toss a cardboard box over it. We practiced our two-step operation so that our synchronization would be flawless. Brush. Trap. Again. . . brush, trap. Emboldened by the simplicity of our operation, we successfully brushed it off the wall, and slammed a cardboard box over the spider—also six inches in diameter, including its legs.

But it was after 9 p.m., and we had to go to sleep, knowing that our operation was pitifully temporary. "What if the spider gets out while we're sleeping?" Jolena asked. "It's not going to get out," I replied. "How do you know? Those spiders are strong! Grandma, believe me. . . it could lift a corner of the box and get out!" she insisted.

Agreed. It's true. I didn't know if the spider's leg muscles could lift a box. So, to give us peace of mind I placed two heavy brass Tibetan healing bowls on top of the box and closed the door to the room. Her mother and a friend happened to be visiting Jeju, and staying in a nearby apartment. We called them for advice. Jolena's mother advised us to ask our friends if there were any superstitions about spiders. Should we kill it, or spare its life and simply remove it from the premises?

Jolena's mom, Elena, made a good point. Jeju's culture has developed over thousands of years as a result of its people's relationship with harsh natural conditions, animistic religion, and mythology. According to Jeju shaman cosmology, all things have a spirit or soul, including animals, plants, rivers, mountains, stars, the moon, and the sun. Each entity is considered a spirit that can offer help or bring harm to humans. As such, spirits must either be worshiped or appeased.

One time, the construction workers on our site warned me about a snake in the garden. "Snake?" I shuddered. "Kill it!" But the worker reminded me that Jeju people would never kill a snake, a very revered and mythological god. If worshipped, one's life will be prosperous. If dismissed, one's life could end up in disaster. On the east side of the island, the Snake God is allegedly stronger. Given the area's share of historical disasters, some men are afraid to even marry women from that part of Jeju.

When my granddaughter's mother came to the house the next morning, she calmly assessed the situation and volunteered to finalize the removal and release of the spider. "Give me a flat piece of board. I'll slip it underneath the box. Then, you help secure the lid while we flip it over."

"Brilliant! Then we can take the box outside and fling it over the rock wall into the neighbor's garden."

What started out as a grandmother-granddaughter operation now became a four-woman counter-insurgency against an innocent arachnid! Elena would handle the lid; I would secure the lid as she flipped the box; Elena's friend, Megan, would open the door; and Jolena would document it on her iPhone. Chris, Elena's husband, watched the entire operation on FaceTime from California. "Wow, this is better than any reality TV show!" Her young son, Tayden, remained clueless. "Mommy, I miss you. I love you!"

After the successful removal of the spider, I was relieved to have spared its life. In the United States, I seldom would think twice about squashing any insect I find in my house. The only exception are crickets. Over the years, I have acquired a 98 percent success rate of catching a cricket in my palm and releasing it outdoors. I've even become accustomed to it hopping around in my loose grip.

Here in Jeju, where the shaman animist beliefs and cosmology are so vast, I am even more aware of restraining my killer-instinct impulses. My friends tell me that since we chose to live in a fishing village in the countryside, we have to co-exist with all kinds of critters, not just snakes and spiders. And if I could welcome them into my yard and home as neighbors, then I can befriend them with a benevolent heart.

Come one, come all. Please. . . just not all at once.

No Beggars, No Thieves, No Gates

I live betwixt and between. The Constitution of my native homeland, America, allows its citizens the right to bear arms. The Constitution of my ancestral homeland, Korea, bans private ownership of guns. On Jeju Island, there is a saying: "No beggars. No thieves. No gates." I find it impossible to imagine a time or place when people didn't ever have to worry about their personal safety or possessions. I've lived most of my life in the US, where there are thought to be about three hundred million guns owned by about a third of the population. That's nearly enough guns for every man, woman, and child in the country.

Gun violence is a woefully expected phenomenon in the United States. One evening when my mother was watching TV in her rocker facing the living room window, a drive-by gunman shot a bullet into the ceiling. It missed my mother—in her seventies at the time—only because her house was situated on a hill above street level. The bullet entered the beams at a 45-degree angle. Another time, she was mugged as she was about to enter the house. Her instinct was to tightly grasp the purse straps against her chest. But in doing so, the muggers dragged and flung her 47-kilogram body down the street, leaving the entire side of her body bruised for weeks. I remember visiting her in the hospital and being traumatized by her injuries.

My husband once participated in an anti-violence demonstration in San Francisco. As a result of carrying a picket sign, a policeman followed him to his car and pointed a gun at his face before hauling him off to jail. We've also been burglarized twice.

Even though our two sons were raised to be streetwise in Los Angeles and San Francisco, I still always feared for their safety. Over a two-year period between the middle of 1979 and 1981, at least twenty-eight African-American children, adolescents, and adults were killed in Atlanta, Georgia. I remember role-playing at home with our sons, David and Tommy, who were then aged six and three. I warned them about temptations and told them to run away from strangers. "Hey little boy, wanna go with me to get an ice cream cone?" Or "Hey little boy, do you like this Star Wars action figure?" There was never any kidnapping. But years later when our younger son was a teenager, he was held up at knifepoint at a video game parlor. Unlike his grandmother, he yielded quickly and gave up his jacket and wallet.

Is it no wonder that when I first arrived in Jeju and heard of the saying "No beggars. No thieves. No gates," I was curious to see if this still played out in daily life, even though it is a saying that originated in a different era. Moreover, I wanted to know how living in a country like Korea, where privately owned guns are forbidden, actually makes a difference in one's sense of personal safety and concern for belongings.

I'm not well-versed in the ongoing debate on guns and violence worldwide. But the debate about gun control is gaining momentum in the United States. I also acknowledge that guns are only one weapon of choice in a very wide spectrum of expressed violent behaviors. Jeju Island is no Fantasy Island, for sure. There are crimes and prisons. But for the most part, we never have to watch our backs as we do in the States. I have frequently walked through dark alleys late at night without fearing for my life. Villagers sometimes still keep their doors unlocked when they leave the house. Car keys, GPS navigators, and smartphones have been left in cars without fear of theft. If you block someone else's car, but leave your cellphone number on the dashboard, the consideration is well appreciated.

We were once told that if a property owner has left an empty field unused, and meanwhile another individual has planted some crops, the owner usually doesn't threaten or remove the occupant. He or she waits until the other farmer leaves. There are self-serve cafés called *muin* cafés around the island. Visitors are beholden to an honor system. After drinking a cup of coffee and eating some cookies, visitors are required to clean up and pay before leaving. Banks provide reading glasses of varying strengths at the counter so that patrons can sign their documents without eyestrain. Even though the glasses are attached to a flimsy chain, I've never seen a chain without the eyeglasses attached.

Times are changing, of course, and Jeju is no exception to the realities of today. Even though there are now locked gates, traditional fences are sometimes seen at the entrance of a property. They serve as barriers for farm animals as well as a means of communicating with one's neighbors. The standard structure includes two stone pillars that allows three wooden logs to be inserted between them. All three logs removed means, "Welcome, we're home." One log in place means, "Returning soon." Two logs in place means, "Gone for a while." And all three logs in place means, "Gone all day—or longer."

Living betwixt and between, I adjust my safety antenna accordingly. If I am in the United States, I am able to relax and enjoy myself once I have taken precautionary measures to guarantee my personal safety. I lock my doors and gates.

I never enter a parking lot alone at night. I zigzag across the street if I suspect someone is following me, and I never leave the house without my husband knowing where I am going. Years ago, I used to carry pepper spray in my purse as a deterrent against potential assault.

When I am in Korea, the main reassurance I have is that I am not likely to ever be shot or held up at gunpoint. This is one quality-of-life measurement and blessing that is disturbingly absent in too many places in the world. If a violent mindset and culture begets constitutional law, then only a non-violent mindset, culture, and vocal movement can transform it otherwise. I dream of the day when children in the United States can attend school like Korean children—without the fear of being shot.

Typhoon Chaba

Autumn in Jeju had finally arrived. Young green persimmons were already turning orange on two of our backyard trees. A cool breeze was more likely to pass through our window than summer gnats. And finally, after waiting months for our clay tiles to be installed on our insulated roof, my frustrations were soon to be abated. Or so I foolishly thought.

The day before our tiles were expected for delivery, village sound systems blared warnings of Typhoon Chaba. Although I had been out during the day, I drove home before dark so I wouldn't be caught in the rainstorm. That night, the wind's fury and harsh voice were so deafening that we cuddled in bed with earplugs. When we woke up, the first thing we did was to look for water that would indicate a leaky roof, and any damage in our garden. Inside, we found a tiny puddle of water. Outdoors, three of our trees—holly, quince, and plum blossom—had toppled to the ground. Even our green onion stalks were bent towards the earth as though someone had deliberately trampled them with rubber boots.

During breakfast, I began receiving text messages and FaceTime calls from family in the US. "Are you alright?" Locally, friends were asking, "How's your house? Any damage?"

It was harder to brace ourselves psychologically for yet another construction delay than the storm itself. But later, I was embarrassed and regretful that I had texted our contractor, Mr. Moon, to come immediately to repair the leak in the roof. Perhaps his own home, his family's, or other clients' had suffered greater damage and losses. He replied: "Tiles delayed because of typhoon. I will come fix the leak tomorrow." Our tiles were presumably stuck on a boat, assuming they had even gotten transported from the warehouse.

It didn't take long before I shifted outwards. We were lucky, for sure. As I walked around the village, I witnessed greater evidence of Chaba's wrath. Locals were already gathering outside and surveying their property damage. An elderly neighbor was grumbling while he swept all the pine needles that fell to the ground. "Look at this, the wind blew off my iron door! All these pine needles. What a mess!" The owners of a local supermarket were planning how they would replace the signboard that now lay as rubble. Several of the stone walls that define village property were also damaged. Big rocks littered the roads. A piece of wood that advertised noodle soup had flown haphazardly off a café wall.

Throughout Jeju Island and the mainland, Typhoon Chaba wreaked havoc as it reached the equivalent of a Category 5 hurricane. The storm left more than 28 centimeters of rain on parts of the island along with winds of 144 kilometers per hour before hitting the southern coast of South Korea's mainland. Busan and Ulsan were most strongly affected by flooding and Chaba's catastrophic winds, with five reported deaths. And I was worried about a minor leak and some onions? My conscience felt even worse after watching TV coverage of Hurricane Matthew in Haiti and Florida, where destruction, death tolls, and the evacuation of millions seemed unfathomable by comparison.

Yeongdeung Halmang, Jeju's goddess of wind and sea, must have been feeling quite stern but benevolent during Typhoon Chaba. Fishermen were warned in time to return their boats to port; there were no reported deaths.

A few days after the storms had passed, we attended a festival in Jeju City celebrating the culture of Tamna, the island's legendary kingdom that existed until it was absorbed in the fifteenth century. Suh Soon-sil, a shaman whom I had met and interviewed years earlier for a book, was performing a shaman ceremony that offered prayers for the safety and protection

of the people. At the end of the event, she spotted me in the audience and quickly ran over to greet me.

"Aaaah, you're here!"

"Yes, I live here now," I replied.

"I didn't know that. You must come visit my home and we will eat together."

She seemed very happy and light that day, more animated than I had ever seen her before. Perhaps, she, too, was celebrating that Typhoon Chaba—the worst in ten years—had quickly passed. There is much more to life than fretting about a leaky roof.

Spirit of Volunteerism

I believe in volunteering. This feeling began during John F. Kennedy's term as President of the United States. On March 1, 1961, Kennedy established the Peace Corps as a trial program. The force would be civilians who volunteered their time and skills to live and work in underdeveloped nations. "Ask not what your country can do for you, but what you can do for your country," he proclaimed. In 2016, the Peace Corps celebrated its fifty-fifth anniversary with more than two hundred thousand volunteers having served in more than 140 countries, including Korea. My brother-in-law, cousins, and niece were among those cadre of global good Samaritans.

I nearly made it to Micronesia as a Peace Corps volunteer in the sixties. After I met Jan in the summer of 1967, he returned to graduate school in Minneapolis, Minnesota, to complete his master's degree in clinical psychology. I wasn't sure if our long-distance relationship would catapult into long-term marriage. But right at the point I was bound for Micronesia, he completed his program and decided to move to California. Within four months, we were married.

Although I never made it overseas as a Peace Corps volunteer, I continued to volunteer over the course of our marriage. After my younger son, Tommy, passed away, I facilitated the local chapter of The Compassionate Friends—a grief support group for bereaved parents. For nearly twelve years, I have also volunteered as an online grief specialist for ShareGrief.com—an Internet-based lifeline for those seeking online support. After receiving so much support during our darkest years, I wanted to honor my son by giving back and helping others who also faced the loss of a child.

After we moved to Jeju Island and built our house in Aewol, my incentive to volunteer was completely different. I wanted to get to know my village community and offer my professional skills as a writer and native English speaker at the local school. I was advised not to volunteer at the high school because the students were too busy with afterschool study halls in preparation for their college entrance exams. Their attention span would be nil. Elementary school-age children would try my patience. So my friend Soonja introduced me to the Aewol Middle School principal who was happy to enlist me as an

English Club sponsor, with the assistance of one of their native bilingual teachers. My only conditions were to meet once or twice a week and include only those students who were highly motivated to improve their English, not those who would view it as punishment.

In Korea, students are taught English as a foreign language from elementary school. But even after years of classroom learning, they often freeze or get tongue-tied at the sight of a foreigner. The idea of losing face or making a mistake is one of the hardest challenges they must overcome. My challenge would be to demonstrate that English as a second language is not only an academic accessory for one's college application, it's plain fun! And most of all, mistakes are OK. I once mistook the word "genitals" for pork at a Vietnamese restaurant. I never made that mistake again.

My group of middle-school students is co-ed. I had forgotten how shy and self-conscious teenage girls can be. They often need prodding to speak and be heard. I was no different when I was their age. One time during high school, I spotted a group of five boys huddled together in the archway where I would normally walk to class. I dreaded walking past them. Instead, I attempted to sprint across the grassy field like a gazelle—only to trip on my own feet and fall on the ground, my skirt splayed across the pavement, kneecaps skinned and brushed with blood. I picked myself up, trying to appear hopelessly nonchalant.

With our English Club, I am careful not to single out any particular student. Through my own experience struggling to speak Korean, I know how necessary it is to be relaxed and free from stress. If the students were adults, I'd offer them a glass of wine. But in lieu of liquor, chocolate is a great antidote for teenage jitters. After snacks, they're well-sugared to chat about books, movies, music, and of course, K-pop.

On one occasion, I invited American novelist and New York Times Best Seller author Lisa See to our club. She came to Jeju Island in order to conduct research about Jeju's women divers. I prepared the students two weeks ahead of time by requiring them to formulate questions they could ask her. Upon meeting her, the girls suddenly became inquisitive. "Why did you write *Snow Flower and the Secret Fan*?" "How do you like Jeju Island?" "What writing advice do you have?" Lisa shared her three top points: (1) Write every day. (2) Write what you love. (3) In the editing stage, remember: The teacher is right; the teacher is wrong; think about it.

Gradually, my students are beginning to show more social confidence. When I bump into them on the street, they shout, "Teacher! Teacher! How are you?" It makes every Wednesday that much sweeter. According to a British study, volunteers have a 20 percent lower risk of death than their peers who do not volunteer. A happier and purposeful life often leads to a longer life. At age eighty, I can reapply to the Peace Corps. They have no age limit for applicants. An American woman named Alice Carter volunteered at age eighty-seven, and served in Morocco. Who knows? I may make it over to Micronesia after all.

Scent of Humanity at Jeju's Five-Day Market

I learned a Korean expression: "*Saram naemsae*," which means "the smell of the people." It's not the same as a putrid body odor. It's the scent of belonging and moving shoulder-to-shoulder among people of all ages. It can apply to those who've come to bargain shop, gossip, eat, and browse at Jeju's traditional five-day markets. Rain or shine, the elderly arrive by bus as early as 7:30 a.m. Many come by car, competing for a space at one of several parking lots. Others are dropped off by taxi. If you live nearby, you simply walk. I usually drive and park the car in my favorite spot so I can enter the market along the entrance and aisle that leads me, past the kimchi and garlic, straight to the organic greens. They are so beautifully stacked and arranged that one expects them to be dealt like a deck of cards. I don't point to the arugula. My vendor already knows why I have stopped by her stall. Her only question is "How many kilos do you want today?"

In the past, Korean markets served as an easy way for goods and services to be traded in one central location in the country's villages. Over time, they grew with cities and towns. In Jeju—and many cities on the mainland—the five-day markets refer to the system whereby each respective market is only open every five days. For example, the largest one in Jeju City is open every day that ends with a two or seven. The closest five-day market to my village is in Hallim, which is open on every day that ends with four and nine. In this way, farmers, fish peddlers, and others can move around the island selling their varied inventory. In order to support the traditional markets, Jeju's local government has even imposed a two-day per month mandatory closure of the large corporate supermarkets. Checking your calendar is a must, lest you miss the opportunity to buy a Korean barbecue pit, a toothbrush, beans, a parakeet, ginseng, and a bonsai pine all at the same place.

No one complains because locals and tourists love to spend hours at one of these bustling cross-sections of humanity. Even if I don't buy more than a bag of dried ferns, no time has been wasted. If I learn the Korean words for brown rice, black rice, and sweet rice, then I will become a more literate shopper. The marketplace is an interactive, voice-driven dictionary.

One rainy day, I took the bus for 1,800 won ($1.50). It wasn't enough just to "smell the people" at the market. I wanted to smell them on the bus as well. Growing up in Los Angeles, we always got around by car. Here on the island, the buses are cheap and convenient—and one can always count on drama! A grouchy bus driver argues the fare with an elderly granny in the Jeju language (the loud granny always wins in a Confucian society). A student vomits in the aisle. A teenage girl preens in front of her iPhone mirror for the duration of seven bus stops. Passengers pack the bus like sardines and you hear five KakaoTalk text message alarms go off at the same time. In unison, scattered voices shout, "*Yeoboseyo*?" (Hello?)

Because of the rain that particular morning, the lenses of my eye glasses were wet. My vision was blurry, so instead of putting two 1,000 won bills in the slot and getting change, I paid two 10,000 won bills by mistake. One extra zero makes a big difference. That's nearly $20. When I didn't get any change, I thought, perhaps, the rate went up. But a few minutes after I seated myself in the back of the bus, I heard ka-ching, ka-ching, ka-ching like a quarter slot machine sounding off in Las Vegas. The man next to me elbowed my side, "Hey, the driver's calling you. Go get your change." Embarrassed, I walked up the aisle, scooped up nearly $18 worth of coins and dumped the heavy load into my backpack.

After I arrived at my stop, I hopped off the bus and opened my umbrella. I spotted my neighbor—an elderly grandmother

—and noticed she wasn't carrying anything but her purse.

"Grandma—hello. Remember me? I'm your neighbor. Let's walk to the market together under my umbrella."

"Oh, it's you. Thank you."

"I'm sorry I can't stay with you because I have to go elsewhere after shopping."

"That's fine," she said. "I will take the bus home."

After we said good-bye, I watched to see in what direction she walked. She moved slowly toward a bench at one of the entrances and sat down before doing her shopping. I proceeded to shop with my list in hand: arugula, iron cleaver, pants, raw crab in soy sauce, and volcanic pumice stones to soften the skin on the heels of my feet. My shopping bag, of course, was large enough to stuff whatever else unexpectedly caught my fancy.

The two market traditions I indulge in the most are bargaining and eating. Some people don't like to bargain. I love to bargain. In my mind, the sale price should be the final result of successful karmic exchange. Like social flirting without the sexual innuendo. I have this one-liner in Korean that goes something like this: "You have really nice things here. I'm not a tourist. I'm an overseas Korean but I live in Aewol Village. If you give me a cheaper price, I will come back again with my friends. Can I have your business card?" Most of the time, the clothing vendors are, of course, flattering. "Oh, that looks so nice on you, Big Sister!" But every so often, there's always

the fussy old man or woman who scolds you for squeezing the persimmons or utters something indistinguishable because you didn't buy the bamboo and wire sifter she was willing to sell for 30 percent off. "*Mianhamnida. Geunyang boneun jung-i-eyo.*" (Sorry, I'm just looking.)

Eating at the five-day market is an exercise in decision-making and restraint. There are food stalls with all sorts of dishes: rice plates and noodles with Jeju pork or blood sausage, steamed corn on the cob, fish cakes, seaweed soup, pan-fried dumplings. My husband's favorite is a greasy tongue-burning pancake (called *hotteok*) filled with hot sesame oil, sesame seeds, and cinnamon, which sells for the equivalent of 60 cents. My favorite eating spot is a large stall located in the center of the market that sells rice cake rolled in the shape of cylinders, served with a spicy and sweet sauce (called *tteokbokki*). Most people order it along with a plate of varied batter-fried sides: green pepper, squid, glass noodles wrapped in seaweed, sweet potato, and zucchini. If you don't shove your way into the crowd and shout out your order in Korean, you'll be easily ignored. My friend and I usually order the rice cakes and sides for only 5,000 won (under $5). Standing room only.

When I compare the experience of shopping in a corporate superstore with fixed prices versus the serendipity of shopping at one of Jeju's traditional five-day markets, I prefer the latter. The superstores are usually air-conditioned, dismissively managed, and stocked with sterile shelves well beyond my height. You can never inhale the breath of four seasons. At the village markets, everything on display is placed at knee or waist height. If you want to inspect the grains in the bin or pick the kohlrabi seedlings you want for your garden, you have to either bend over or squat. The vendors are engaging. Self-service is never an option. At Jeju's traditional markets, I revel in the scent of humanity. It's worth sniffing every five days, even by bus for $20.

Spirit of Sasam,
Jeju's April 3 Uprising and Massacre

One of my neighbors is a poet and artist. I met him through a woman who lives in our village. Upon learning that I was a writer, she insisted on making the introductions to Kim Jong-ho, who grew up and lived in Aewol Village for most of his life. He was born in 1939, nine years before what is known as the April 3, 1948, Jeju Uprising and Massacre, or Sasam (sometimes written "4·3").

When I first visited Jeju Island in the 1980s, I was unaware of this dark historical period. Like most tourists, I was initially awestruck by the aquamarine waters, the prominence of Hallasan Mountain, the rocky cliffs of Seogwipo, and the scalloped-rimmed horizon of smaller volcanic cones. It took several visits before I discovered that underneath the veil of scenic beauty were layers of genocidal atrocities.

According to the Jeju 4·3 Research Institute, the brutal suppression by the police and military forces against armed rebellion in Jeju occurred between 1948 and 1954. Many factors led to the massacre: social unrest after World War II as independence took hold after thirty-five years of Japanese colonial rule, the Jeju people's anger toward the government's administration, abusive Japanese police officers, co-stationing of the local and national army with a US military presence, and a controversial election after the partition of the peninsula in 1945 that eventually led to separate governments in the south (Republic of Korea) and north (Democratic People's Republic of Korea).

Not until January 2000, when a Special Act was decreed by former South Korean President Kim Dae-jung calling for an official investigation of this period, were numbers recorded of how many Jeju residents were massacred during the incident (eighty thousand) and the number of villages destroyed (more than half of Jeju's four hundred). Since then, detailed reports, articles, and testimonies have become available to the public. In 2008, bodies of massacre victims were discovered in a mass grave near Jeju International Airport. Excavations continue around the island to this day.

My neighbor, Mr. Kim, explained that most of his knowledge was based on oral history, stories passed down by relatives and elders who were actually victims and eyewitnesses. But what he saw as a child remains indelibly marked in his memory.

"I was a second grader at the time. When there was violence between the people and the police in Aewol, we could hear guns firing. My mother hid me under the persimmon trees and covered me with a blanket," he said. "But I was too young to understand what was going on."

Due to a strong labor and leftist movement in Jeju, the island was perceived as a Communist threat to establishing the Republic of Korea under Syngman Rhee. Student intellectuals—including those from Aewol—studied in Japan. Upon their return, the police considered them as agitators. Mr. Kim said that most of the intellectuals accepted Marxism-Leninism and brought their theory back to Jeju.

"People in the same village had different ideas. One person who was targeted as a leftist escaped by boat. The police came and asked the doctor why he let his assistant go. So the doctor was arrested and killed. The police went to the mountains to find other guerillas. When they were captured, they were beheaded. Their heads were put on public display in the village. It was a warning. I saw the heads myself."

Many guerillas escaped to Hallasan Mountain, he said, but would come down to get food from their villages. The police forced the locals in the villages to build a wall with thorns and forced them to stay inside. That way, they could prevent the insurgents from being aided by the villagers. If villagers were suspected of being related to insurgents, they were captured and killed by virtue of association, regardless of their age or gender.

According to one woman in Bukchon—a village that suffered greater losses than others—many of the atrocities took place at the playground of an elementary school. "Many of the grannies who survived the massacre used to visit me and recall their memories. They said the soldiers would come to the village, set the houses on fire, and force the people to stand in rows at the school while they were being shot on suspicion of being a Communist or associated with the insurgents."

Jeju people were not involved in the ideological matters, said Kim. "It was a fight between the Russian Communists and the Americans. Korea was caught between two sides. Innocent residents are always the ones who are sacrificed."

Each year, a Sasam commemoration is held at the Jeju 4·3 Peace Park. When I first began coming to Jeju on a regular basis in 2007, I was able to attend one of the ceremonies. Five thousand elders and others arrived by bus and were seated in an orderly manner before a stage and altar lit with incense. After the official speeches, the attendees were led up to the altar where they lay white chrysanthemums in honor of their loved ones who perished during Sasam. Many of them paused with tears in their eyes.

If they were in their seventies and eighties, they would have been youngsters and teenagers at the time of the massacre. Like Mr. Kim, their understanding of Sasam would have been steeped in narratives told by their families and neighbors that explained the actual atrocities, collective grief, and chaos they witnessed. Several decades have since passed but artists and poets like Mr. Kim still ponder the earlier years that influenced their lives today.

When I first met him, he shared a poem that he wrote entitled "Swaying." With his permission, I have translated it below, as it poignantly captures the sense of being in Jeju.

Swaying

Moment to moment
Living is like swaying without end

How much more must we struggle
To flow like a long river
In this windswept world
How much more should we sway
Like winds dragging the sky

Hummingbirds labor for a drop of honey

Flapping their wings eighty times a second
Flowers become flowers
Pushing their frozen dreams
Underneath the winter's earth

Moment to moment
Becoming a human
I am forever swaying.

Sister Rosarii McTigue's Legacy

Hallim is the third largest urban center on Jeju Island and closer to Aewol than the capital of Jeju City. It takes us ten minutes to drive there, compared to thirty. We drive there often for the local five-day market, to get our hair cut, buy stationery supplies, and stop by Baskin-Robbins for an occasional ice cream cone. But the first time I ever visited Hallim was in 1987. Were it not for an interest in textiles, I never would have learned about a legendary Irish priest in Jeju Island, and an extraordinary Irish Catholic nun. Since living on the island, I have been fortunate to meet both. Their legacy is a reminder that one doesn't have to be a native to contribute to the island's economic and social well-being. I think of them often, especially as I navigate the course of my life here.

The former—Father Patrick James McGlinchey—first arrived

in Jeju in April 1954 at age twenty-six. Poverty was rampant after the Korean War, and he earnestly sought to help the locals make better use of their natural resources. The son of a veterinarian in Donegal, Ireland, McGlinchey knew something about animals and farming. But whenever he spoke to the elders, they would always reply: "*An doemnida.*" (No, it won't work.)

"Farmers," he said, "are the most stubborn people in the world. For five years, I did nothing but speak to people. But it was all a waste of time. I was a foreigner. They thought, 'What does he know?'"

When he realized he was getting nowhere with the adults, he began to organize the youth into 4-H clubs and teach them how to feed and better raise their pigs. Upon his initial arrival, he was shocked to discover that the locals raised their livestock in their own outdoor toilets; a practice, he said, that began with the Mongols who occupied Jeju in the thirteenth century.

Everywhere on the island he observed mentally disabled children, presumably afflicted by trichinosis. When the locals ate poorly-cooked pork that came from pigs fed on human excrement, the tiny worms infiltrated the human brain.

Since Hallim was a fishing harbor, he instructed the youth to bring back the fish heads and parts that the fishermen were throwing away. "Protein is very important for the pigs," he said. Without protein, Jeju pigs could live for three years and still never reach fifty kilograms. "I saw clover everywhere along the side of the roads. We taught the kids to mix together the raw fish, clover, and barley rice."

As he began to teach the locals more about cattle raising and organic farming, he eventually established St. Isidore Ranch, which is also highly regarded today as a horse stud farm. With the income from the sales of the farm's organic milk, cheese, and beef, McGlinchey also established a clinic, a nursing home, a hospice center, a youth center, a retreat center, and a daycare center. For his contributions to Jeju Island, McGlinchey was recognized with the highest national honor, the National Recommendation Award, at the presidential office in December 2014.

Lesser known, however, is another project that Father McGlinchey championed in the 1960s. He pondered how he could improve the economic livelihood of the thousands of Jeju women on the island. After persistent appeals to the Columban Sisters in Magheramore, Ireland, McGlinchey was able to convince Mother Mary Gemma to dispatch three Irish nuns to Hallim to develop a woolen mill that included weaving and knitting of traditional Irish Aran Island sweaters. Sister Rosarii McTigue was one of the three Catholic nuns who arrived on Jeju Island to establish Hallim Handweavers in 1962. Joining her venture were Sisters Brid Kenny and Elizabeth Taaffe.

When I first visited the Hallim Handweavers in 1987, Sister Rosarii may have been there at the time. But I have no recollection of meeting her then. I purchased one of the wool sweaters, knitted in the traditional Aran Islands style, and a blue, green, and fuchsia plaid shawl. For years, these hand-woven and hand-knitted pieces unraveled memories and a longing for Jeju Island. It wasn't until twenty-five years later that I actually inquired more about the history of Hallim Handweavers. I visited the priests of the Columban Brothers in Jeju City in 2012 and learned the names of the nuns who actually managed the mill projects. "Where are the nuns now?" I asked.

Upon discovering that Sister Rosarii was living in Magheramore after she left the island in 1999, I wrote to her and asked that she share her memories of Jeju and of working with the young women of Hallim Handweavers. After all, she had spent thirty-six years of her life here. Even though the original Quonset huts of the mill have been replaced by a building now used by the church that McGlinchey built in the 1950s, I can still hear the clacking of the looms. I can also get a glimpse of what it was like for Sister Rosarii to live here, based on her own words:

> The Hallim Handweavers was a daring vision and a tall order for anyone who would respond to Father McGlinchey's need.

Those of us undertaking the project would have responsibility for directing the project from the time the wool arrived at the mill, through the various steps of weaving, and on to the sale of textiles and garments in shops both nearby and far afield. Father McGlinchey would provide the wool and attend to the finances until such time as the venture would become self-supporting.

Public transport in Jeju was minimal at the time of our arrival in 1961. More reliable was the parish jeep, especially for taking long journeys across the island. We fell in love with the small ponies peculiar to the island, and marveled at their flowing tails, winsome faces and dainty steps as they grazed in the wild or took their burdened journeys along difficult tracks.

The site for the handweaving industry lay just a short distance from our convent. Father McGlinchey had provided accommodation for our work in the form of five Quonset huts. With a loom provided by the United States Overseas Mission, local carpenters built three small looms and fifteen larger ones. Water, without which the industry could not even begin, was obtained through the help of a water diviner. The Irish brother of one of the Columban fathers was shown a picture of the site proposed for the weaving. With his divining equipment in Ireland, he located a spot on the site where a powerful spring could be found. So it happened that water was found. . . (and the project was then underway).

One of the most difficult things a missionary must do before moving away from any mission is to say good-bye to the people amongst and with whom she or he has spent a number of years. So it was with Hallim and me. For

thirty-six years, I had watched the people of the neighborhood and far beyond develop a prosperous way of life
through their work in the weaving industry. Together with
my companion Sisters I had thanked God to see both women
and men develop skills which would enrich their way of life
and that of their families. I had seen children make progress
in education thanks to the earning of their parents both on
the site of the weaving and through the products created at
home. I had been enriched by the friendship and loyalty of
those with whom I had spent my energies, trying my best to
always give witness to the values of the Gospel and always
from the cultural values inherent in the Korean way of life.
I hold in my heart happy memories of relaxation days with
the staff when we went off to some special place and enjoyed

time together as we sang, danced, and told stories. Hallim Handweavers was not all about work!

* * *

It hadn't occurred to me that I should go to Ireland to meet Sister Rosarii. At first, I was simply delighted to know that she was living peacefully in Magheramore, a small hamlet in the eastern county of Wicklow. But one of my friends piqued my interest by pointing out that the Aran Islands, off the western coast of Ireland, were very much like Jeju. Both islands are subservient to the wind; both have stone walls meandering throughout their respective landscape; and both make use of an abundance of seaweed, albeit for different reasons. In the absence of fertile soil, Aran Islands farmers create seaweed-and-sand beds in order to cultivate potatoes. My friend also recommended that I watch the film "Man of Aran," a 1934 Irish fictional documentary directed by Robert J. Flaherty about the harsh life on these three islands. "You will see the similarities with Jeju," my friend said.

After watching the film, I began to connect more dots. Since the Hallim Handweavers' textiles were patterned after the Aran Islands, why shouldn't I make a trip to Ireland to meet Sister Rosarii in Magheramore—one hour south of Dublin—then visit her place of birth, note the mills where she learned how to teach weaving, and travel to Inishmore—the origin of the Aran Island sweaters that Jeju women replicated for their economic survival. I wrote to Sister Rosarii, "Please remain in good health. I am coming to Ireland to meet you."

In preparation for my trip to Ireland in 2013, I visited the former site of the former Hallim Handweavers and met one of the Catholic church staff. She told me that during her missionary stay, Sister Rosarii had extended her generosity and compassion to a young disabled woman. In those days, many people suffered from tuberculosis and polio. The woman, now in her eighties, didn't have a family to take care of her. So Sister Rosarii had allowed her to live in a small space of the parish. They both kept in contact and called each other every Christmas. I visited the woman's home, and she gave me several photos to take with me to Ireland. "Please give these to Sister Rosarii."

I made the trip to Ireland with my husband, Jan, and Han Youngsook, my translator and interpreter for *Moon Tides—Jeju Island Grannies of the Sea*.

In the autumn of 2013, we arrived at the Missionary Sisters of St. Columban in Wicklow. Jan was wearing one of the Aran sweaters that his brother had bought decades earlier. He wanted to delight them with proof that the handwoven sweater had lasted over fifty years! I brought along the plaid shawl that I purchased at the mill in the 1980s. We also remembered to bring the disabled woman's photos and a copy of *Moon Tides* so Sister Rosarii could enjoy the images and stories of the *haenyeo*.

Upon receiving the book, she turned each page slowly, as though she was examining swatches of silk. Different photos touched upon a memory. One of them showed the *haenyeo* wearing cotton bonnets. "Oh, we had hats like this, too," Sister Rosarii said. I told her that I had grown up hearing that "Koreans were the Irish of the Orient." Did she agree? "Yes, I think there are similarities in our attitudes toward people—friendliness and generosity. We both laugh a lot, cry a lot, sing and dance a lot," she continued.

The nun sitting nearby added that "Koreans suffered like the Irish. And for that, you still get something beautiful." A photo of women wearing persimmon-dyed clothing further caught Sister Rosarii's attention. "That's typical clothing for Jeju. You won't find that on the mainland," she said. She appeared so alert, engaged, and open-hearted. It wasn't hard to imagine how respected and well-loved she must've been among the young Jeju women. Given her own musical background and studies at the Royal Academy of Music in Dublin, Sister Rosarii must have been as irrepressible as Maria, the singing nun portrayed in *The Sound of Music*. In addition to her Christian beliefs, she had to be quite feisty in order to survive Jeju's post-war conditions and the island's willful natives.

After chatting, we were escorted into the cafeteria. Rather

than sitting down, Sister Rosarii briskly rushed off to fill our trays. Another sister chased after her. "Sister, please sit down with your guests." Stepping in closer to me, the protective Sister whispered into my ear: "Oh my, she is simply beside herself today—too excited!" As we sat together eating our lunch, Youngsook and Sister Rosarii and a few of the other nuns spoke in Korean. I was impressed that they could still understand and speak the language. Several of the other nuns in the cafeteria came up to greet us and tell us that they, too, had served in Korea and enjoyed the Korean cookies delivered to them each Christmas.

Our visit with Sister Rosarii was no more than two hours. We didn't want to exhaust our welcome. When we said good-bye at the entrance of the retirement home, we gave each other warm hugs. I knew I would never see her again. But a few months later, I knitted her a blue green mohair scarf and mailed it to her for Christmas. She sent me a Christmas note with postcards of nature surrounding Magheramore.

As her health declined, we were unable to maintain a regular correspondence. She died on October 22, 2015, after suddenly becoming ill. The Sisters in Magheramore had received a message from Father McGlinchey remembering that she had never been in a hospital during her entire life, a testament to her strong will and spirit until her final days.

Sadly, Jeju's history books may not include stories of her

long-term mission. Visitors to St. Isidore Ranch, however, can view a permanent exhibit of the Hallim Handweavers, including the original loom that Father McGlinchey's father shipped from Ireland to Jeju Island as a prototype. Under the devoted tutelage of Sisters Rosarii, Brid Kenny, and Elizabeth Taaffe, the Hallim Handweavers once employed eighty women who worked in the textile mill and 1,300 women who knitted the Aran Island sweaters in their homes across the island—most earning money for the first time. Due to Sister Rosarii's marketing skills, the Hallim Handweavers products gained enough of a fine reputation to be sold in the Chosun Hotel in Seoul. Locally, orders were also received from the Korean Navy and US Peace Corps volunteers.

In 1999, after thirty-six years of missionary service, Sister Rosarii returned to Ireland. After her departure, the woolen mill eventually closed its doors. In spite of its termination, there is still evidence of this significant past. Whenever I drive from Aewol to Hallim's downtown, I can easily spot the visible steeple that identifies the Catholic parish that once shared the factory grounds. Each time I wear my Aran Island sweater, I think of Sister Rosarii, the indefatigable Irish nun whose presence in my life was like a moonbeam—ephemeral and far-reaching.

* On April 2018, Father Patrick J. McGlinchey passed away on Jeju Island. His remains are buried at Isidore Ranch.

Peace on Jeju Island

Ask me where I live, and my face cascades into a smile: "Jeju Island." Simply murmured, these four syllables elicit an inner peace. Depending on the inquirer, the dialogue may continue. "Isn't that the place where the older women free dive?" I am not surprised that this designated "Island of World Peace" has become synonymous with the *haenyeo*, women of the sea. But what many people don't realize is that the *haenyeo* are more than divers. Their legacy includes a fierce advocacy for human rights and environmental protection. Facing struggle has always been as natural as holding hands.

Given my history of social activism since the 1970s, I am always searching for ways to support global peace, particularly in Korea. In 2017, I was invited by the Jeju Peace Forum Secretariat to participate on a panel honoring the *haenyeo* because they had been recognized in 2016 by UNESCO as Intangible Cultural Heritage of Humanity. The invitation was given on the basis of my book *Moon Tides—Jeju Island Grannies of the Sea*. It was timely because the *haenyeo*'s livelihood—now at risk—is so inextricably bound to environmental sustainability and world peace.

All the panelists were storytellers. Each one had been invited because they had documented the culture and spirit of the free divers in their own way: through oral history, film, photography, and the written word. The *haenyeo* continues to draw the attention of domestic and foreign media. In my speech, I explained that when I began research on my book, I knew very little about these women. I was, of course, awestruck by their ability to free dive as older women. But over the course of my fieldwork, I learned more about their multi-faceted lives as mothers, farmers, community workers, and environmental activists.

When I actually began writing my book, I used a metaphor that would capture the fluidity of their lives. It was the "tides" because the *haenyeo*'s diving schedules and safety are regulated by the moon. Also, Koreans observe significant events such as the autumn harvest and ancestral rites according to the lunar calendar. So I visualized these women's hard lives as being "lifted by the winds and tides" of economic survival, love of family, and hope for the future generation.

In my closing remarks, I made a plea for the Jeju Provincial Government to launch an on-going, seashore clean-up program whereby all of Jeju's elementary, middle, high school, and college students would be required to participate in trash elimination and conservation activities. In this way, the youth could better honor the *haenyeo* and protect the environment for their own future.

Like most first-time visitors to Jeju Island, I, too, was initially attracted to the central presence of Hallasan Mountain, the undulating landscape, and its coastal villages. I still become mesmerized watching the waves curl and bend toward the shore—engaged in supplicating bows. In this way, Mother Nature reminds us to be humble and grateful for its majesty.

But these days, I lament the vulnerability of the island. What I didn't expect was to witness the fleeting nature of the virtues that seduced me to live here. Now, these virtues are frequently referred to as endangered, and local villages have become rallying points for protests against excessive development, the desecration of shaman altars, forced eviction, and feared militarization.

In spite of growing apprehension, I still feel very blessed to live on this tiny dot floating in the sea. But I pray for greater dialogue and transparency between nations, governments, and the people. If it takes a village to raise a child, then it takes a movement to protect an island.

Years from now, the sound of these four syllables, "Jeju Island," must continue to echo clarity and conjure peace.

Meditation at Bogwangsa Temple

It was one of the noisiest weeks ever. Donald Trump had just won the presidential election. Text messages, Facebook postings, FaceTime chats, and media coverage—ad nauseam—were adding volumes of stunned and vitriolic voices to living rooms worldwide. A powerful earthquake had rocked New Zealand, triggering a tsunami. In North Carolina, the Ku Klux Klan was preparing victory parades.

There was no escape from havoc, even on our remote volcanic island of Jeju. And yet, my husband and I chose to unplug for just one day—to re-center and quietly commemorate what would've been our younger son, Tommy's, thirty-ninth birthday on November 13, five days after the 2016 election that shook the world into political uncertainty.

We were seasoned mourners since our son had died of

cardiac arrest on February 16, 1994. This was when the US president was Bill Clinton. In that special week of February— twenty-two years ago—people in America were listening to "The Power of Love" by singer Celine Dion. Now, fans of Canadian songwriter Leonard Cohen were commemorating his passing by pondering the layered meanings of the words to his elegiac song "Hallelujah."

Before we actually unplugged that day, I posted a photo on Facebook of a nearby temple with the message "Heading here to contemplate world peace." One of my friends, Tim Shorrock, replied: "Let us know what you conclude." So off we went to Gonaebong Oreum, one of Jeju Island's 368 smaller volcanic cones that is located very close to our village in Aewol.

Jan had first discovered this spot by bicycle. Knowing that I grimace when it comes to biking uphill, he first brought me to this location by car. I loved the spot immediately and designated it as the perfect place to be on Tommy's birthday with our friend Han Youngsook and her son, Seongmin. We parked our car and began walking toward Bogwangsa Temple. I am not a Buddhist by any means. I was actually raised as a Methodist; my grandfather was a minister. And yet it felt very comfortable and healing to sit cross-legged on the temple pillows in silence, the four of us.

I asked Youngsook, a native of Jeju and student of Buddhism, to explain the pink lotus lanterns hanging above our heads.

They are iconic in many Korean temples. Each lunar year during Buddha's birthday, people flock to the temple and offer wishes, she explained. Their names are written in Korean on a white strip of paper that adds length and breeze-drawn movement to the paper lanterns. They remain hanging from the ceiling for one year until they are removed and refreshed the following year. I like the idea that they are not permanent.

Between one year and the next, attendance will inevitably differ, as will the wishes. I continued sitting quietly, formulating a private wish that I could breathe in for the moment.

After our meditation inside the temple, we walked up the trail passing numerous mounds of graves covered with grass. We noticed that some upscale gravesites were enclosed by a ring of shallow stone walls. Others were situated in undelineated spaces. Some were marked with upright headstones. Youngsook said that these days, more Koreans are leaning toward having their remains cremated, space being an expensive and waning commodity. As we viewed these graves, she spontaneously turned to her son and instructed, "Don't do anything fancy for me. Once I'm gone, I'm gone." He quickly reacted, "When I die, scatter my ashes everywhere."

From higher ground, we could view seventeen other volcanic cones that defined the bulbous landscape. These geological formations are unique to Jeju. Hallasan—South Korea's highest mountain— will always command the central attention and reverence of the island. Its history and myths abound. But without the gentler slopes and at least one hundred hills with trails and poetic names like Dragon's Eye, New Star, Hundred Herbs, and Moon-like, there would be no undulating landscape for sojourners to feel underfoot.

After we returned home and I logged back in to Facebook, I wrote my conclusion for Tim. I replied: "Sitting daily in quietude with Mother Nature opens the heart." I made a resolution that day to listen more seriously to those whose views are different from mine, that I might become a better hunter of common ground. Whining and becoming cynical is not an option.

No question that social media has been one way for family and friends to express themselves and engage each other. But nothing replaces the gift of tangibles. As we descended the trail back toward our car, the fire watchman called out to us. "Before you leave, please take this." He handed us a branch with four ripe tangerines. We thanked him for this friendly Jeju custom of offering visitors the island's citrus. I slipped them into my bag with sixteen pine cones I gathered from the ground, one for each year of my younger son's brief but tangible life.

Language of Compassion

Someone once advised me that learning a foreign language is easier and faster when lessons are based on your interests. If you love food, begin with the word *siksa*. It means meal in Korean.

All during my childhood, language and food were as inseparable as egg whites and yolk. My grandmother lived with us when I was growing up in Los Angeles. Since both of my parents worked full-time, she was the chef of our kitchen for breakfast and dinner. For lunch, we would either take our tuna sandwiches to school in lunch pails, or eat in the cafeteria. I loved Thursdays   anticipating the routine menu of hamburgers and Jell-O with whipped cream. Dinners at home were often Korean and American food served together: rice, romaine lettuce salad, steamed broccoli, fermented cabbage, and a roast leg of lamb. Before the culinary term "fusion" became popular, we were already mixing and matching. The day after Thanksgiving, we didn't make turkey sandwiches like our other American friends. Koreans made rice porridge with the meaty carcass, and topped it off with sesame oil, soy sauce, and freshly chopped scallions.

I particularly loved my grandmother's Bisquick pancakes for breakfast. She assumed that the way to prepare them was the same as the way she fried her Korean seafood pancakes. The edges were always crispy in both because they were cooked in a generous pool of Crisco shortening—long before the popularity of cold-pressed extra virgin olive oil. To this day, I won't eat a pancake unless it's thirteen centimeters in diameter and crispy around the edges like a Korean flapjack.

When my grandmother wasn't cooking, she also took it upon herself to teach me and my sister the Korean alphabet—both written and spoken. As teenagers, we were sent to summer school at the local Korean church to improve our proficiency. Years later, I hired a private tutor and also spent eight weeks in Bloomington, Indiana, during an intensive language program sponsored by Yonsei University. Even after all previous attempts to learn Korean, I still knew more food vocabulary than varied grammatical sentence structures.

The turning point came with immersion. After we began living in Jeju for more than one year at a time, I noticed that my Korean improved markedly. When in the company of my predominantly Korean-speaking friends, I have no choice but to listen, respond, imitate, and ask questions related to the subject under discussion. If your friends share common interests, then your chances of understanding the conversation is even better. Thus, I have friends who are writers, painters, textile artists, filmmakers, designers, teachers, and chefs.

One of my Korean-speaking friends owns a café. I met Youngsoon one day while Jan and I were biking along the coastal route in Gwideok, the village where we lived before moving to Aewol. Her café caught our eye because it was constructed out of a metal container, a popular and affordable trend in Jeju. As we approached the restaurant, her dog, named Happy in Korean—barked so loudly that Youngsoon rushed out to greet us. We became friends instantly because we both love the sea and enjoy cooking. I showed her my book on Jeju divers, and she told me that her mother worked as a *haenyeo* before she died. Youngsoon inherited the land from her mother and established the restaurant and seaside pension a few years ago.

I've eaten at her restaurant on many occasions. One of my favorite dishes is hot steaming rice, topped with fresh sea urchin. When Youngsoon prepares seafood pasta, you know that the octopus was caught by the local *haenyeo* on the same day. The greens in her salads—lettuce, arugula, and cilantro—were grown in her garden. Jeju's tangerine adds a sublime twist to the oil-vinegar dressing and her herbal teas.

One day, Youngsoon showed me a cookbook of Korean vegetarian temple food. Like a whistling kettle, I couldn't help but voice an idea. Why don't we teach each other English and Korean through food? We could meet every week for breakfast and use her restaurant as the setting for bilingual conversation. She loved the idea, and we began to meet every Tuesday morning, before her customers arrived at the door.

I began teaching her how to greet foreign customers in English: "Hello, welcome to my café. My name is Stella. Please have a seat here. Would you like to see a menu? Make yourself comfortable and I will be back to take your order." Also, "If you need to use the restroom, it's outside over there."

A few weeks into our lessons, another mutual friend, Eunjung, asked to join us. She and her husband own an art gallery in the Artists' Village in Jeoji. Each time we met for breakfast, I prepared something that they may not have tried. One time, I made a hummus dip. They learned the words "Middle Eastern," "blend," "chickpeas," "tahini," "cumin," "paprika," "lemon," "olive oil." I learned the same words in Korean. Another time, I shared some leftover Thanksgiving dressing and a green Peruvian dip. And so it went every week. Stella would bake a frittata; Eunjung brought fruits, such as rare red kiwi. We exchanged phrases like "bon appétit" and "*masitge deuseyo.*" What we've discovered is that the food is simply an appetizer before our meatier conversations about life, death, aging, marriage, and children.

At one point in our conversations, we realized that all of us had experienced the unexpected loss of a loved one. Stella's father had died in a motorcycle accident when she was twenty. Eunjung's first husband had died in a helicopter crash. And I had experienced the loss of my younger son, which I wrote about in my memoir, *Seaweed and Shamans—Inheriting the Gifts of Grief.* They both wanted to read the translated version

of the book in Korean. Since I only had one such copy in Jeju, they took turns reading it. In one of the essays, I wrote about the comfort I had received when two different Mrs. Kims brought me seaweed soup at two separate times in my life— once after the birth of my first son, David, and once after the death of my younger son, Tommy.

After reading my book, Stella announced that she would prepare seaweed soup for our next breakfast and language class. "I want to make it for our own healing," she said. The following week, while we savored the silky ribbons of kelp floating in the warm broth, we could taste each other's sorrow. We offered each other compassion in silence, without any need for bilingual translation.

Epilogue

At the time we began building our house, we were uncertain how much time we would spend between the US and Korea. Jan had obtained his permanent residency status, which meant that he could avoid the inconvenience of leaving the country after his three-month period without a visa. But in order to retain his status, he would have to be in Korea at least once every two years. Given our attachment to living and working here, that requirement would not pose a problem. I, however, was still subject to the limited three-month restriction until our friend Jay Kim reminded me otherwise.

One afternoon, I mentioned that I might have to leave Korea again in order to obtain a new visa. Fortunately, she recalled that I had told her that in 2013, my grandfather, Rev. Yim Chung-koo, had received recognition as a national patriot by the South Korea government's Ministry of Patriots and Veterans Affairs. "Did you know that as the descendant of a

patriot, you can apply for Korea citizenship?" she explained. Soon after confirming the good news, I actively pursued this legal course of action and eventually received my dual citizenship in 2016. Ironically, what began as a practical means to circumvent the visa limitations created an unexpected entry point to learn more about my grandfather's legacy and to contemplate how to live as a twenty-first century global citizen.

Very sadly, I never knew Rev. Yim Chung-koo, who was born in November 1887 and died in December 1939 at age fifty-three, nearly a decade before I was born. I only knew that he was a minister for over twenty years at the Korean United Methodist Church in Oakland, California. It wasn't until I met Professor Cho Kyu-tae of Hansung University in Seoul that I even realized how actively he supported Korea independence during Japan's occupation. Cho had learned of my grandfather's religious and political activities with the Heungsadan

(Young Korean Academy, founded by fellow patriot Ahn Chang-ho) while conducting research before the church celebrated its centenary in 2014. He was the driving force behind my grandfather's patriot award.

When he asked me where my grandfather was buried, I had no idea. But after I searched my mother's old files, I found a stack of receipts from a florist that annually provided flowers for his gravesite at Mountain View Cemetery in Oakland. My cousin Gail and her husband, Norm, who lived in Oakland, volunteered and found not only my grandfather's gravesite, but that of his widowed mother, Choi Seong-deok. My great-grandmother left Pyongyang in northern Korea with her son, bound for America aboard the SS Siberia in 1905. Over the course of the next thirty-four years, Yim Chung-koo would receive his bachelor's degree in economics from University of California, Berkeley, a bachelor's degree of divinity and a master's degree at Pacific School of Religion, and actively continue his religious and political activities until his death.

As we continued constructing our house on Jeju Island, I began thinking more about global citizenship than I ever expected. We could not have settled in this fishing village without having built relationships based on respect, loyalty, and mutual tolerance for our neighbors, our contractor, the workers, and the community of Aewol.

However, these values were actually imbued within me

before we even broke ground. Global citizenship began with my grandfather who immigrated to America. It was there that he received his higher education, met my grandmother, and raised a family in California. He always kept Korea independence in his heart without having to reconcile living in one country and supporting another.

In my case, dual citizenship and global citizenship have required me to deeply ponder their relevant distinction and relationship. The former requires social and legal responsibilities to two specific countries. But global citizenship in the twenty-first century requires me to view a broader screen in which to define my moral values. It is a philosophical mindset that transcends time and place. No matter where I am living or traveling, building a spirit of community begins with humbling face-to-face encounters, however uncomfortable or fearful they may be. These are the simplest and truest building blocks for creating world peace today.

I would like to believe that Rev. Yim Chung-koo is looking down approvingly at our expanding global family. We are no longer one homogenous tribe. The Yim family probably includes more than eight grandchildren, fourteen great-grandchildren, and fifteen (and counting) great-great-grandchildren of mixed heritage from many countries: Korea, China, Germany, Japan, nations of Europe, Mexico, and the Philippines. We are one segment of an infinite necklace of human faith.

Acknowledgements

Hyekyoung Ahn: for talismans and continual cultural guidance.

Hind Baki: for encouragement to write only what feels right.

Kyu-tae Cho: for gifting my grandfather's legacy.

Youngsoon Choi and Eunjun Kim: for meals, art and language lessons.

Dahlia Gerstenhaber: for sharing a mutual passion for the *haenyeo*.

Youngsook Han: for finding our property, liaising with our contractor, and being by my side at any hour.w

Mikyoung Kang: for honoring us in our home during Chuseok season.

Shinhwan Kang: for constant care and attention while we lived in Gwideok.

Kyounghee Kang and Keun Lee: for loving nurturance and practical and aesthetic construction advice.

Jong-ho Kim: for sharing Aewol history.

Seungeun Kim and Jee-eun Lee: for their island enthusiasm and our food club adventures

Soonjin Kim: for her green thumb in our garden.

Father Patrick McGlinchey: for recollections of Hallim Handweavers.

Sister Rosarii McTigue: for her spiritual and resilient character.

Kyeungsook Min: for tender house-sitting during the summer of 2017.

Jung-hwan Moon: for managing construction of our house with care, patience, taste, and humor.

Jolena Pamilar: for a most memorable summer together and house moving assistance.

Giuseppe Rositano: for insights on shamanism and Jeju culture.

Lisa See: for writer's inspiration and a shared moment together in Jeju

Thu Kim Vu: for creative listening and post-manuscript R&R in Taiwan.

Soonja Yang: for urging me to write before it's too late and for introducing me to her native island and world of textiles.

Kwangsook Yim: for being my sidekick and companion in the sea.

Hank Kim and Misoon Yang, my publisher and his wife, for their steadfast faith in my projects and encouragement to discover my truths.

Eugene Kim, my editor, for her insightful comments and broader perspective that kept me on track. And Todd Thacker for his meticulous copyediting eye.

There are also those—near and far—who knew of this project and supported me continuously with their love. Thank you. You know who you are.

Jan, my life partner: for keeping our marriage as improvisational as jazz. And David, our son: for adding syncopation.